Re-
Competitive
Strategies

Re-Competitive Strategies

How to Regain Growth Profits for Mature Businesses

Mack Hanan

American Management Association

This book is available at a special
discount when ordered in bulk quantities.
For information, contact Special Sales Department,
AMACOM, a division of American Management Association,
135 West 50th Street, New York, NY 10020.

Library of Congress Cataloging-in-Publication Data

Hanan, Mack.
    Re-competitive strategies.

    Includes index.
    1. Product management.   2. Product life cycle.
3. Competition.   4. Corporate profits.   I. Title.
HF5415.15.H35   1986   658.5   86-47588
ISBN 0-8144-5888-2

Printing number

10 9 8 7 6 5 4 3 2 1

To **Bob Cujē** and **John Fischer**
  Who had more than their fair share
Of mature businesses
  Yet who had more than their fair share
Of corporate courage
  To restructure them with me
Into recompetitive brands

Preface

This book is about recompetitiveness, and the strategies in it are based on the following two very important questions:

1. *Where is business growth most likely to come from?*

The most predictable type of growth comes from making established, mature business recompetitive. More venturesome growth approaches are progressively less predictable. The most aggressive growth strategies are the least predictable. This says something to companies that want to grow. Manage a broad spectrum of growth strategies, from conservative to venturesome. But for the surest, quickest, and most cost-effective growth, make mature businesses recompetitive.

2. *How can you tell when the time has come for recompetitive strategies?*

It is time to become recompetitive when a product line has become indistinguishable from one manufacturer to another. It is time when technological advantage has disappeared. It is time when patent protection has expired. It is time when cost increases can no longer be passed along to customers as higher prices—and when cost savings must be passed along to customers as lower prices instead of being retained as higher margins. It is time when new investment in your asset base will never reach your hurdle rate but there is no choice if you are to stay even with the competition. It is time when you consider the sale of an aging business, but you find that the employee severance costs, facilities writedowns, and cost burdens transferred to your remaining businesses are simply not affordable. It is time when diversifications you have effected to reduce dependency on cyclical commodity products have created losses instead of gains. If your business is experiencing one or more of these symptoms, then it is ready to become recompetitive—and the sooner the better.

Contents

Introduction

All of us in this generation of management have been programmed with an incorrect model of the business life cycle. We were told that maturity follows growth. In reality, maturity is built into growth and is an intimate, and far too early, part of it. We were also told that after maturity there is decline. This is not necessarily true. There is an alternative model; it says that after maturity there can be recompetitiveness, a rebirth of growth.

The profits from recompetitive growth can, and most of the time do, exceed the profits from new growth, in their rate of return and very often in their volume as well. Since their investment is mostly bought and paid for, and if we are careful not to add too much to it, the savings from cost reduction and the incremental earnings from increased sales can drop virtually unimpeded to the bottom line.

The tail end of the life cycle turns out to be just as profitable a place, if not more so, to apply growth strategies as the beginning. It is also a whole lot less risky. Everything we deal with—product, market, and competition—is already known. Rejuvenated profits flow quickly. No new sciences, no new channels of distribution, no new markets need to be waited on. In many cases, results begin by the ninety-first day.

When growth strategies are applied to mature businesses, a magical transformation takes place. The market becomes the focus of attention, not the product or its competition. Profit replaces volume as the single most crucial objective. Profit center managers and the sales force work together in teams, abandoning their adversary roles. Managers who have been working with their heads down, thinking up new ways to tweak productivity or titillate motivation, pick their heads up and go into their markets—not their laboratories or plants—where the sources of their new profits reside.

As a matter of professional practice, I take a perverse pleasure in saying something like this to managers of mature businesses: "You are leaving money on the table. There is undeveloped profit in your business, money that represents a failure to capitalize fully on your asset base, money that you have already bought and paid for. How do I know this? I base it on one fact: Your business is mature. What if you can improve the profit contribution of your business by a mere 1 percent over the next twelve months? How many dollars of new earnings would that represent?" In a mature business of leadership size and share of market, a mere 1 percent is a huge number. Yet I have a 99 percent level of confidence that it can be achieved.

Why the 1 percent hedge?

There are two reasons. Over the past decade, I have encountered exactly two businesses that could not be restructured into sufficiently improved profitmakers to justify the effort. So impossibility exists, usually because the technology of the business is so obsolete that its product becomes irrevocably noncompetitive. The 1 percent hedge allows for this. The second reason is a good deal more prevalent. It has to do with management.

Mature Managers of the Old School

In most mature businesses, the most mature component is the manager. And he—it is almost always a he—is found just where he imposes the greatest constraints on recompeting: in the very businesses that are the most mature and that can benefit the most by a rebirth of profits. The airlines were, through the 1970s, run by leather-helmeted, eye-goggled, open-cockpit pilots; as someone said, they remembered everything there was to remember about "how to flew" but knew all too little about how to manage a business. They had, and still have, their replicas in other industries: the former stock and bond salesmen who run the brokerage houses, the traditional bankers who still believe that their product is money, the brewers who are more at home stirring the vat than stirring the market, and the engineers who abound in managing all the science-based businesses that make hardware.

These managers are the hardest to move toward recompetitiveness. Part of the reason is that they know so well how to do what they have been doing: selling commodity products in volume at whatever margins they can wring from the market. The other part of the reason is that they do not know what they have *not* been doing: partnering at high decisionmaking levels with major customers, selling profits rather than products, and basing price on the value of the profits they sell instead of on competitive prices or cost. To say that they are risk-averse is to miss the point. They prefer to accept the 100 percent risk of ever-declining margins to the 99 percent probability that they can be reversed.

Every industry has its old school. They and their businesses have grown mature together. Some managers yearn for the past, hoping it will come again. Others hold back the future. And at least one of them carries the corporate memory, the sum total of recollections of all that has been tried and failed when it went against the tried and true. If a business is old enough, everything will probably have been tried. Therefore it will not need to be tried again.

In the automobile companies, the old school waits for the return of six-passenger, full-size sedans. Petrochemicals old-schoolers wait for the next cycle of demand, hunkering down until their overcapacity will again come into play and hoping in the meantime that one of the industry's major competitors will drop out—but not them. In high-technology businesses, the old school devotes itself to building a more perfect product while the markets they serve need more perfect applications from their existing products and more perfect realization of a positive return from their original investment.

In such circumstances, managers like these tell me, who needs to bite the bullet of recompeting? "We ain't plowin' half as good as we already know how," they say.

Yet there is always someone who will declare himself—and, increasingly, herself—and come forward for growth. In the Du Ponts, the General Electrics, the Hewlett-Packards, and the 3Ms of the world, managers here and there are restructuring their businesses. They are showing their companies a model of profit renewal in a business that, in the defeatist language of the 1970s, came to be known as a cash cow to be milked or a harvest business to be picked clean before it withered in the fields. With restructuring, their business and the corporate concept of its culture are being revitalized. And so are they.

What if a mere 1 percent of your managers do likewise?

The Magic of 1 Percent Restoration

What if you could restore the competitiveness of only 1 percent of your mature products? What if, by doing so, you could improve their net margins by a mere 1 percent? How much incremental profit would that mean to you just this year alone?

Your answer is the absolute minimum value you can add by *recompetitive strategies*—by rejuvenating a mature commodity line of business into a fighting brand once again, no matter how far along it may be on the life cycle curve, how imitatively its performance benefits have been equalized by competition, or how much pressure is being exerted on its price.

What is the magic of 1 percent? It represents a bare minimum, selected for dramatic effect. Although minuscule, it converts to a significant infusion of new earnings for any mature product with a sizable share of its market. The rate of return on these new earnings can be much higher than on new products, except the one in ten that makes it big. Yet, unlike new products, the restoration of competitiveness in mature products requires a comparatively minor investment that is rewarded by an almost immediate payback at exceptionally low risk.

In terms of quick, dependable new profits, no investment can match the revitalization of a mature business. These dollars are available to most of us right now. Yet we are leaving them to lost opportunity. Either we do not know that they are there or we do not know how to get at them. When we try, we do exactly the wrong things. We do the very things that have made our products mature in the first place. We employ the conventional wisdom, "rouging the cheeks of the corpse" by growing unit sales in every way we can: enhancing our products, selling harder to current customers, expanding sales to new customers, and entering allied markets. We add costs to an already top-heavy asset base. We fail to recover them when we buy business with low margins. Meanwhile, of course, our competitors do the very same.

Maturity is the equalizing of differentiation. When maturity comes, margins shrink. It is not our competitors who shrink them, but our markets. They speak to us through our margins. They tell us that our performance benefits have been replicated: They have been homogenized by competition or trivialized by a more emergent technology. *Maturity occurs when we lose margin control.* When customers set our margins, it is they who are marketing to us. It is we who pay the price.

A mature business, by definition, is marked by a level or declining demand. Growth, if it occurs at all, is at the replacement rate. Price differences identify the competitors. Other forms of differentiation, most of them minor in their effect on price support, are provided by service, deals, and marginal benefits such as packaging. Resource conservation is the order of the day. Losses may be impossible to recoup. Return on investment can be maintained only if investment is cut to the bone.

Maturity is the time in a product life cycle when the business must readjust itself to its market. Its original adjustment has become obsolescent. The value-to-price relationship of the business has gotten away from management's grasp. The market sees the value it is getting as too low for the price it is being asked to pay. Or, as it is more often expressed, price is seen as being too high. If we do not readjust the value to make it higher, the market will readjust the price by making it lower.

At maturity, we cannot readjust value by tinkering with performance. Our competitors will not allow us a period of grace to develop and market new, breakthrough performance values. They will be right on top of us, replicating what we do increment by increment. They have the same needs that we have. They also have the same capabilities. At maturity, none of us can use performance as a long-term, or even intermediate-term, leg up on readjusting product value. Only by moving to a different type of value—customer financial value—can we hope to create new user worth that will once again give us command of premium margins.

The Coming of Realization

The universal first reaction to maturity is denial. Even sophisticated managers are not immune. In 1979, mainstream product line earnings at IBM declined for the first time in 30 years. IBM's immediate reaction was to find reasons why the decline would be only transitory. It found seven probable causes:

1. Inflation
2. High interest costs
3. Aggressive competitive pricing
4. Unfavorable currency exchange rates
5. New plant startup costs
6. Soft economy
7. Slowed market growth

All these events were real; they all existed. But none was the real cause. Earnings were declining because the product lines had become mature.

Necessity is the mother of perception. We see what we need to see. The converse is also true: we do not see what we do not need to see. At B. F. Goodrich in 1981, it was said "We are just now seeing market maturity that we should have seen five to seven years ago." In fact, the tire business had become mature many years earlier. New names for old brands, new features and benefits, and price-off promotional strategies had heralded maturity for over a decade to everyone but managers in the tire business.

At Goodyear, they were saying well into the 1980s, "The way to make money in the tire business is to make more tires."

Maturity, or at least its realization, also came to Du Pont seemingly "all at once." Many of its commodity businesses, such as polymers, fibers, and agricultural and industrial chemicals, matured simultaneously. Du Pont had held on to them too long. Only in 1985 did it discontinue its methanol business, which had provided ever-decreasing margins for over two decades. "We can purchase methanol now for less than we can produce it," Du Pont said. Since 1981 alone, prices had fallen 35 percent. Because the Methanol Syndrome was pervasive throughout the company, Du Pont had to adopt a familiar three-part strategy: (1) it improved some product lines and sold them harder; (2) it bought another mature business (Conoco, for $7.8 billion); and (3) it made minority investments, buyouts, and joint ventures in other industries—electronic data storage and imaging, blood chemistry instruments, and life science technologies based on "living polymers." In none of these businesses can Du Pont ever again expect to own 50 to 100 percent of a market over life cycles of half a century or more.

This same pattern of late reaction and stereotyped response can be seen at Xerox, another company that, in the words of Irving Shapiro, former chairman of Du Pont, "didn't know where the end of the rainbow was." For a decade and a half, starting in 1959 with the Model 914, Xerox owned the plain-paper copier market. Its name became the synonym for office copiers. Then, partly as a result of its own success, market growth for large copiers slowed. Xerox had become mature.

Xerox refused to consider small-niche markets of less than $100 million a year in gross revenues, and thereby abdicated the personal copier business to the Japanese. It can never compete there. Because of the same mass-market focus, Xerox has turned down new products developed for it by its Palo Alto Research Center that have proved highly successful as foundation businesses for Apple Computer and several other companies. Lacking new copier products, Xerox tried to migrate into electronic data systems. It has become the computer industry's most conspicuous failure, losing hundreds of millions of dollars on unmarketable word processors, printers, filing systems, and work stations for the Office of the Future.

Xerox has also tried diversification, buying into the financial services industry through a $1.5 billion acquisition in property and casualty insurance. Xerox profits have been reduced still further by the acquisition. Now, in addition to competing against the Japanese in copiers and against IBM in office automation, Xerox is in a third highly competitive industry that is also mature.

In its original business, Xerox has reacted in typical ways. It has cut prices, reduced costs through layoffs, and increased automation and outsourcing of components to cheaper foreign suppliers. At the same time, it has added to its asset base by increasing its investment in "exciting products" for office automation. It is earning less money and spending more, the classic bind of a mature business.

Nongrowth Generic Strategies

What can we learn from Goodrich, Du Pont, and Xerox? Each of them adopted the traditional coping mechanisms of maturity:

1. Refusing to downsize mainstream business, even in the face of a slowed rate of market growth.
2. Rejecting smaller high-growth markets based on their total sales volume rather than their potential profitability, resulting in the failure to implement demonstrably successful new product developments. At the same time, growth market niches have been abandoned to the Japanese and other Far East competitors.
3. Betting the future of the business on industries already highly competitive among dozens of other companies, including the Japanese.

This portfolio of Not-to-Do strategies is a primer for noncompetitive maturity. It reveals the historic lack of preparedness for the inevitability of maturity and an ignorance of its signals or an arrogant assumption that they do not apply. This is the infamous Not Applicable Here Syndrome. It leads managers to reject strategies that can restructure a mature product line, not on their merits but because of cultural affinity to volume-based instead of profit-based businesses. Xerox summarizes its strategies as "a number of mistakes." Actually, they are the cookbook solution, the basic order of battle when maturity sets in and traditional management principles are applied.

Three generations of American managers have been taught to manage mature businesses by "milking" them; perhaps *harvesting* is a more genteel term. As a result, they have become overdependent on old products and on the same old strategies for marketing them:

1. *Product renovation.* Add marginal performance differentiation to the product.
2. *Technology licensing.* License engineering expertise to competitors and potential competitors.
3. *Sales pressure.* Sell harder by selling something to everybody at any price, regardless of cost of sales or margins.
4. *Cost leadership.* Become the low-cost producer in order to offer the lowest price as a result of experience-curve economies of scale.
5. *Market share dominance.* Achieve a high customer base to absorb volume production regardless of profit.
6. *Service emphasis.* If the product cannot be differentiated, make service abundant and distinctive regardless of its cost and give it away to help justify price.

Strategies such as these have a near-perfect track record— they almost always fail. They are inherently flawed because no business can add more to its costs than to its earnings and survive, let alone prosper. Product renovation adds to cost. Selling harder adds to cost; the cost increases with volume. Free service adds to cost and subtracts from margins. Service cost also increases with volume. The low price affordable by being a low-cost producer

Figure I-1. Product life cycle.

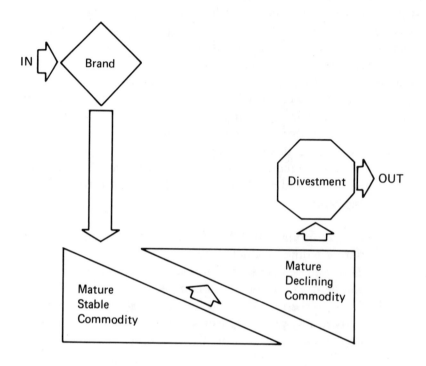

encourages volume. Yet low-margin volume cannot repay the costs of renovation, sales, and service and still return a competitive profit.

Along with generic strategies, there is also a generic mindset. It is based on having cake and eating it too: on combining growth and cash generation at the same time. Union Carbide's petrochemicals, metals, and carbon businesses are mature. Its mindset toward them is symptomatic. "We really expect these businesses to grow," Carbide says. "But they must grow in the framework of generating cash."

Like all aging processes, maturity is inevitable. It is part and parcel of growth: its endpoint. Maturity is implicit in every successful product life cycle. As Figure I-1 shows, products that start out as brands—that is, products that can command premium price based on premium value—eventually become stabilized by maturity. Stability, unless turned around, leads to decline and, generally much too late, to divestment. While the cycle may be prolonged or attenuated, it cannot be denied. The sole question is *when?* The answer is, earlier and earlier. This means that the need to plan the restructuring of competitiveness has become permanent. Every major line of business requires it. Otherwise no significant asset buildup will ever be justifiable.

The Onrush of Maturity

Maturity is an onrushing fact of business life. And it is setting in earlier in the life cycle than ever before, lurking just beyond the breakeven point in many cases and not much farther above it in others. There are three major reasons why the rate of maturation is rising, why the mean time between market entry and commodity status is shrinking. They are reasons of our times. They come out of the new rules that we are all obliged to play by in the latter part of the second half of the twentieth century.

1. Maturity overtakes businesses earlier today because the rate at which new technology is being applied to commercialize new products and services has been speeded up significantly over past decades. More pure research is initiated with commercial applications in mind. The time between invention and application has been condensed. Stronger pressures are being put on research and development (R&D) to be more "productive." This is business code for technologies that can be put to work in the marketplace as soon as they leave the lab. In companies whose "market derivation" is more mythical than real, R&D is seen as the source of differentiation that can justify higher margins. At the very least, R&D is expected to permit a lower manufacturing cost per unit or ensure sufficient volume even at low margins to make profits.

2. New sources of foreign competition are a second cause of early maturity. The global economy has far more players, and far more sophisticated players, than the old so-called international

economy that preceded it. Globally, it is not only knockoffs that are foreshortening the growth phases of life cycles. Technology jumps now come from a broader base of competitors. So do lower labor costs. Many American businesses operate at a 30 to 50 percent disadvantage compared with foreign labor. In addition, they are frequently outclassed in productivity by as much as two to one. Much of this burden is the legacy of structural costs that were allowed to build up over the good years when inflationary price increases covered up for indiscriminate staff and asset build-ups.

The influence of faster technological application and competitive replication, often at lower price, is shown in Figure I-2. Its upshot is startling. No longer will a business, regardless of its industry or market, be able to depend on long life cycles for its products. In the past, life cycles have often run for half a century or more after market entry and have provided not only the cash foundation for the business but the very definition of the business itself. Short, fast-growing S-curves, periodically restructured into competitive positions, will now be the rule. Even newly founded businesses in the highest technologies will not be exempt. In less than five years, Apple Computer grew from nothingness into a multibillion-dollar business. Within that time, it became mature. It had trouble developing new products in its increasingly bureaucratic structure. And it had trouble selling its mainline products, eventually being forced to close its factories because of "an oversupply of computers brought about by sluggish sales." Unless management learns the strategies of restructuring and implements them relentlessly, this will be the fate of every business.

3. There is a third cause of earlier maturity. Major corporations have become commodity-ridden, infested with me-too products and services. As a result, they have developed a particular genius for maintaining mature businesses over prolonged periods of time, letting down their positions on the life cycle curve slowly and with consummate grace. Indeed, this skill has become the basis of their strategic doctrine. So imbued with it have they become that even new businesses are introduced to their markets with commodity strategies that feature the product, extol its performance benefits, and attach price to the product in the same

Figure I-2. Factors accelerating maturity.

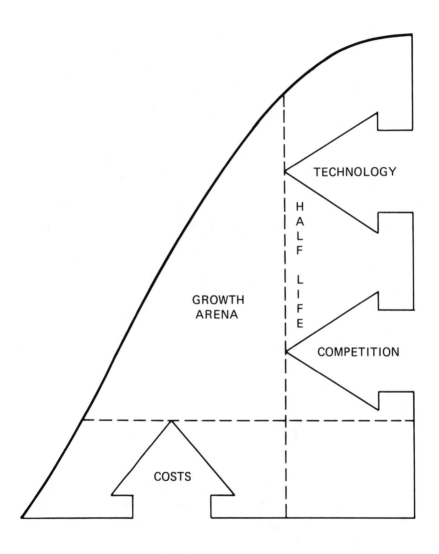

way that makes it vulnerable to competition in older lines of business. New products are born old: they are mature from the inception, selling on price-performance and inviting margin erosion at the hands of both rival producers and customers.

The Three Rules of Recompetitiveness

The progressive margin shrinkage of noncompetitive maturity can be avoided. Competitive maturity, with its regrowth of margins, can be planned for. The slide valve industry is a classic example. It goes back a long way, to the ancient city of Pompeii. Even in 79 A.D. a complete line of slide valves in all sizes, shapes, and varieties was apparently available; they are preserved in the ruins. In modern terms, they were in commoditylike profusion. Clearly, sometime before 78 A.D., the slide valve industry had become mature. Since then hundreds of models, then hundreds of makers, have competed. One company, Xomox, has profited the most. "We make valves," Xomox says, "but we market applications." Their competitors, however, make valves, market valves, and tie their margins to valves.

Mature products challenge their customers in the wrong place. They go head to head with customer cost containment. Mature products base their price on cost and their sales strategy on adding less to cost than their competitors. Since no cost can ever be cheaper than no cost at all, customers exert pressure on all attempts to add any costs at all to their businesses. This is especially true if customers are themselves mature. Because commodity products no longer have differential performance advantages to play off one against the other, price is their one remaining option. Customer cost containment forces their option downward. To be different means inevitably to be cheaper.

No product can profit in the spiderweb of customer cost control. To be competitive in maturity, a product must escape from being perceived as an added cost to be controlled and enter its customers' profitmaking system. It must become perceived as an added source of profits, not costs. When this transference is made, customer pressure will reverse itself. No longer will it press downward. It will go the other way, seeking to maximize new profit contribution. The customer will want more new profit, not less. When he receives more, he will pay more. The product, although still mature, will become competitive again.

The message of maturity is loud and clear: *Profits can no*

longer be based on confronting customer cost control. Supplier profits must be based on improving customer profits.

This message sets the three cardinal rules for achieving competitive maturity. They are derived from the recompetitive doctrine in Appendix A. Each rule contributes to our ability to improve customer profits and thereby our own. Each rule therefore violates everything we have learned about how to manage a commodity business. This is the litmus test that allows us to prove each rule. If it is not in violation of traditional mature business management, it will drive us only deeper into low-growth, no-growth margins. It will not restructure our business; it will not make us competitive again.

The first rule is *market concentration*. Mature markets, which are markets that have grown fat, must be leaned down to the customers whose profits we can best improve. These will be customers with operating costs that we can reduce enough so that profits can be significantly improved or customers whose profits can be improved by sales or productivity increases we can help them achieve. These customers will compose our growth niche. They will be our "growables." To the extent that we can help them become more competitive, they will drive recompetitiveness for us.

The second rule is *asset base shrinkage*. Product lines that have proliferated along with their markets must be downsized. The products that remain will be of two types: those that can best contribute to improved customer profits, which will become the mainstays of our competitive maturity, and frank commodities that can still be profitably mass marketed by us if we use stringent cost-effectiveness.

The third rule is *product redefinition*. Instead of enhancing the product, we must displace it with a new offering. The new offering must be the product's ability to improve customer profits. The physical product, which we customarily regard as tangible, must be replaced by a financial product—the dollar benefits the product offers to customer businesses. These are the only true tangibles in any business transaction. Nothing else can be put in the bank. When profits instead of products are offered, price can be detached from product benefits and attached to their dollar benefits. Since dollar benefits can be differentiated even after product benefits have been homogenized by parity, price can regain its upward elasticity.

The Perpetual Branding Machine

Mature commodity businesses are typically capital intense. For this reason, they require a high operating rate and low-cost production. Costs and cost-effectiveness become prime concerns. The lowest-cost producer has an advantage. Over the business life cycle, which has traditionally been lengthy, management can react slowly and thoughtfully to the major decisions that affect long-term earnings. To be a "good manager" of a commodity business means to be good at three decisions: how to manage volume so that investment in new facilities can be timed just right, when and how to introduce marginal product renovations, and when and by how much to reduce price.

To be competitive at maturity, however, requires a new set of skills.

At the outset, it must be understood that the capital asset base of the business is no longer its growth base. It is, more often than not, its liability. Volume capacity is no longer a blessing. With its depressing effects on price, it is frequently a curse. Downward price management, continually trading margins for market share, becomes a vestigial talent. The premium shifts to premium pricing. The asset base shifts to a customer database, which now becomes the growth platform for the business. Adding value to customer businesses, far more than adding production to inventory, becomes the business's drive force: not getting products out the door, although that is still where they have to go, but getting profits added to the bottom lines of customers. The ability to add new profits to customers, not product performance distinctions, is the new source of differentiation.

This new type of differentiation has a name. It is called "branding": adding value that can command a premium price.

The ability to brand—and, in the case of recompeting, to

rebrand—is the paramount capability for profitmaking. It is therefore the best test of a manger's proficiency. How well does a manger brand and rebrand? That is the question. There are two ways of answering it. One is based on how well he or she managers original brand development to retain present competitiveness, as described in Appendix B. The other, which is crucial for purposes of regaining competitiveness in maturity, is based on the management of brand marketing.

1. *The Brand Development Test.* The mean time between the development of successive brands is the first test. The shorter the mean-time interval, the steadier the brand stream and the more consistent the flow of premium profits. A short mean time suggests that management has discovered the formula for growing its business. It has learned how to grow customers by supplying them with premium values so that they will, in turn, support their supplier with premium price.

2. *The Brand Marketing Test.* The mean time before a brand's decline into commodity status is the second test. The longer the mean-time interval, the greater return on the brand's original investment and the more impressive the accumulation of total profits. A long mean time suggests that management has developed a proficiency in marketing that allows maximum "hang time" for its branded businesses in their customer use patterns. During this time, the brand maintains its premium value. It therefore retains command of premium price because it continues to be the best grower of customer profits.

The optimal time for developing brands is always now. The generation of new S-curves, new life cycles for emergent streams of profits, must be perpetual if the mean time between curves is to be short. In this sense, a business is a perpetual branding machine. If it stops producing brandable products and services, it falls into irreversible maturity. A slowdown in branding gives the same effect. The rule of thumb to follow for high scores on the Brand Development Test is always to have one brand concept in development while another is in the market and a third is being regenerated: "one in the freezer, one on the table, and one in the oven."

Just as there is an optimal time to stock the freezer with

potential new brands, there is also an optimal time to regenerate an existing brand's S-curve by restructuring "in the oven." The time to restructure is always earlier than we like to think. Figure I-3 shows the optimal time for applying recompetitive strategies. This is the S-Curve Regeneration Window. It comes much sooner in brand life than the traditional half-life point, which is reached well after the life curve has slipped off precipitously.

Normally, there are four requisites for a branded business. It requires a *growth value* to deliver to the marketplace, a *growth driver* to manage the strategy for adding the value to the market, a *growth organization* to support the driver, and a *growth market*. When a commodity business is to be rebranded—that is, turned around from maturity to a growth mode—the same requisites pertain to it; there are no free lunches in growth. Three of the four can be managed. The fourth requisite, a growth market, may be impossible to obtain in maturity. If it does not exist, we will have to simulate its growth by growing our customers who are in it.

The Regeneration of S-Curves

Recompeting mandates born-again strategies. It also imposes on us a new vocabulary like the one shown in the Recompetitive Dictionary in Figure I-4. Old words, and the concepts they speak for, must take on new meanings. Otherwise, the business will remain mired in commodity-speak, a position from which it can neither preach nor practice recompetition.

Being "born again" as a competitive line of business is going against the grain of the product life cycle. To give a mature life cycle a new S-curve, only an eclectic strategy can produce restorative results. The strategic keystone is a redefinition of the business. It will take a new mission statement to guide a commodity business back to growth. Old-style mission statements such as this classic—so flatulent that they are actually *emission* statements—will no longer do:

Figure I-3. Optimal application of restructuring strategy.

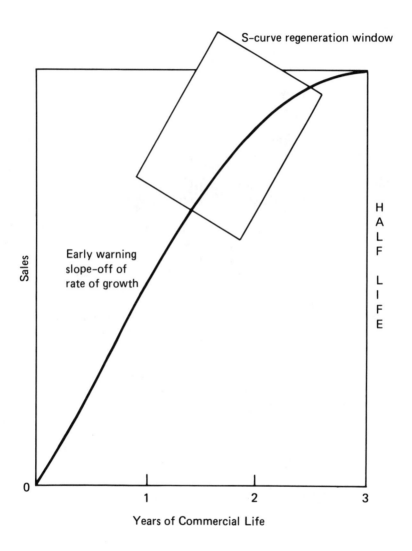

Figure I-4. Recompetitive dictionary.

Maturity	Competitive Maturity
<u>Mission</u> is to manufacture and market high-quality products.	<u>Mission</u> is to grow new profits for customers.
<u>Objective</u> is market share leadership and to be low-cost producer.	<u>Objective</u> is to be leading profit-improver for customers.
<u>Customer</u> is someone to sell to.	<u>Customer</u> is someone to grow and be grown by.
<u>Market</u> is everyone with a need for the product.	<u>Market</u> is customers who can be grown most cost-effectively.
<u>Product</u> is hardware or software.	<u>Product</u> is improved customer profits.
<u>Price</u> is the cost to a customer, justified by product performance.	<u>Price</u> is an investment by customers in their growth, measured by return on investment.
<u>Selling</u> is persuading customers of the best price-performance benefits.	<u>Selling</u> is consulting with customers on the best profit-improvement benefits.

OLD

To achieve competitive excellence by manufacturing and marketing quality products and services.

In order to grow, we need a growth mission. It will have to dedicate us first to the growth of businesses other than our own so that their growth will force growth back upon us:

NEW

To grow selected electronics manufacturers who are already being grown by us or who are growable by us so that their profits are improved by the application of our systems of business management expertise, market and competitive information, products, and services.

Growth Partnering

To be competitive in maturity, we can grow only by growing our customers. In competitive maturity, we grow by segmenting out our growing and growable customers from all others and concentrating on them. In competitive maturity, we grow by becoming expert applications specialists, not hard-selling product vendors; by making customer data our pivotal resource, not our traditional asset base of sunk costs. If we cannot make these adaptations, we will be noncompetitive in maturity and premature in falling off the end of our life cycle. We will be leaving significant sums of earnings unrealized, almost all of which have already been bought and paid for. We will have forsaken cost-effective growth.

The effects of mature growth can be electrifying on our own people, galvanizing them into a renewed dedication with some of the devotional frenzy of a garage-type startup. Mature growth can also mesmerize our competitors. But most of all, becoming competitive once again in maturity can provide the explosive incentive our customers need to recreate their own growth.

More than anything else, it is our customers' growth that propels our own. To become a growth business, a mature product must have a growth market. To the extent that it provokes that market, provides its incentive, counsels its strategies, and partners with its growth managers, a mature business underwrites its own rebirth.

Whether maturity is a new beginning for premium profits or their swan song is in our customers' hands. In our mutual best interests, we must do everything we can to join hands with them. Their accelerated growth, and our hand-in-hand regrowth, must take place in parallel.

The selection of the customers we will grow is the single most important decision we can make in restructuring our competitiveness. If we are wrong here, we will be wrong everywhere. If we choose to grow customers who are not growable by us, or who are not *the most growable* by us, we will have no one who can grow us. It will not make any difference what else we do right. Without improving customer profits, we will be unable to attach premium prices to our contribution. Without premium pricing, we cannot regain competitiveness.

Accurate customer selection depends on accurate market knowledge. This is historically the weakest area of mature management. Commodity business managers know their product far better than they know their customers' products. They know their competitors far better than they know their customers' competitors. They know their own costs far better than they know customer costs; their own operations far better than they know customer operations and where costs cluster within them; their own distribution far better than the distribution channels of their customers. This lack of customer knowledge—knowledge of the customer, by the customer, and for the customer—is the greatest impediment to recompetitiveness.

AT&T is overcoming the impediment by databasing its business on an industry basis, selling growth profits instead of PBX switches and basing its prices on the amount of profits it can deliver rather than on its delivery of the switch. RJR Nabisco sells packaging materials on the basis of their ability to help customers grow. At 3M, mature businesses dealing with mature markets are putting aside their product systems and getting deeply involved with the customer operations they affect. They are proposing new profits instead of new products, working as partners instead of vendors, and showing results of millions of dollars of incremental earnings for their customers as well as for themselves.

The classic case of all is IBM. One IBM customer, Black & Decker, gained $15 million in sales through forecasting with an IBM online database. Sales lost by the unavailability of merchandise were reduced. At the same time, employee productivity was increased by 24 percent. H. J. Heinz, another IBM customer, increased the order entry productivity at Heinz USA by 75 percent and saved $200,000 with distributed processing. As far as Black & Decker and Heinz are concerned, IBM does not make computers—IBM makes customers more profitable. The computer business is essentially a commodity business. But IBM has branded its offering, displacing its product in favor of customer profits, and receives brand-type profits in return.

Each of these companies has discovered the essential truth about making money in business. Profits slow down and stop at maturity, which occurs when our customers' growth stops or when it proceeds independently of us. Profits speed up again when we restructure our business to help customers grow again and to make our joint growth a partnership, interdependent once more.

I
CONDENSE

1

Brand the Business

Making a business recompetitive begins with condensation. The business must be shrunk to the core products and services that can be branded—that is, offerings that can be endowed, either once again or for the first time, with the capability of commanding a premium price.

Brandable products and services may be current brands, perhaps suffering from undermarketing. In that case, their margins can be raised. Or they may be commodities that can be rebranded. The financial effect of their operating values can be translated into premium user values that will pay users back for a premium price.

The core lines of business that can be branded will form the basis for recompeting. They will be the heart and soul of the restructured business. Other slow-growth or no-growth businesses will require a stay-or-go evaluation. Cost-disadvantageous businesses whose technology has been superseded or whose labor content has become noncompetitive are candidates for divestiture. The capital employed in them can be rescued and reallocated to the brandable businesses, strengthening them with internally generated funds. Many mature businesses, however, are slow growing or cyclical yet still able to throw off desirable cash flows. If they can be managed so that their asset bases are more fully exploited, their profitmaking contribution can be significantly increased. Best of all, their new contribution can be generated with little or no incremental investment.

When a business is reduced to its brandable core, it takes on many of the attributes of a newly born growth business. It is smaller, more comprehensible in terms of its lines of business and their markets, less burdened by high, unreclaimable costs or overheads, and dedicated anew to high profit achievement. It will be a lower-volume business, serving a reduced share of market. But because it will be branded—because it will command superior margins—it will be able to earn higher profits on less volume. At the same time, it will be free of the overbearing cost structure that accompanies volume-driven businesses. Higher earnings on a reduced asset base provide the ideal return-on-investment formula for growth.

Taking Command of Premium Price

At the outset of competitive restructuring, the one correct question is: How can we earn growth profits on a lower annual volume? Asking it will invariably lead to branding, which is the one correct answer because it is the key to premium unit margins. It is the sole strategy by which less can be sold for more.

Otherwise, business managers can easily delude themselves into thinking they are restructuring when they are actually ensnaring themselves in the volume trap all over again. As they see their markets becoming mature and their products falling into commodity status, supply seems to be everywhere while demand shrinks or stays the same. Some managers ask the wrong question at this point: "How can we get a larger share of the smaller pie?" This leads to price wars with already depressed margins and the increased costs of sales to "sell something to everybody" regardless of profit. Survival on that basis can be emotionally rewarding, but from the standpoint of growing the business in hard dollars, it is an empty victory.

Branding is the key to accelerated growth. Branded businesses and products are premium earners of growth profits because they and they alone can command premium price. The definition of a brand is based on this unique distinction: *A brand is a commander of premium price.* Growth businesses are businesses that have one or more price commanders in their mix.

Branding is not merely naming a product or trademarking it with the maker's signature and seal. That would be too easy. After all, commodities are also called by name. A brand, defined in capital-generating terms, is a product whose perceived economic value is noncompetitive. So superior is its perceived value that no competitive product or business can match it.

It is an understatement to say that a brand's perceived premium value justifies a premium price. In reality, a brand's perceived premium value *requires* a premium price; or, said in another way, it *commands* its price.

To equip a business to be a price commander, its products must be perceived by its market as offering unsurpassed economic value. The genesis of branding lies in this perception. To grow a business at an accelerated rate, it must be brought to branded status as quickly as possible and held there, in command of premium price, as long as possible. This guarantees its contribution of premium profits.

Price command opens the door to profit leadership. It also permits the competitive isolation of a business. Rivals who try to erode the business's franchise by price cutting run the risk of reducing their own profit on sales. They also may underscore the price commander's superior perceived value by their contrast. In effect, they act unwittingly to validate the brand's claim to preemptive value. They tend to make commodities of each other, often leaving the price commander in sole possession of the market perception of premium value.

The Brand Formula

A brand is a resolution of two forces. One is premium price. This rates a brand's performance in terms of what it does for its supplier. The other is premium value. This rates a brand's performance in terms of what it does for its customers. These two variables must be in a specific relationship with each other for branding to occur. The customer must receive a premium value in order to justify a premium price. The price can be high, even ultrahigh. But the premium value must be perceived as being even higher.

Marketing is the principal branding function because it is the sole corporate mission with the capability of creating perceived value. True enough, value must be present in the transaction before it can be perceived. But value is often present without ever being perceived. Conversely, genuinely superior value is not always present and yet a premptive value of some sort is nonetheless perceived. How does preemptive value enter the perceptions of a market? In every case, marketing puts it there.

For a market, perceiving is believing. If a market perceives preemptive value in a product, the belief is that it is there. The converse is also true. Many premature commodities suffer from disbelief in their preemptive value. Many mature commodities can be rebranded if market belief in a regenerated preemptive value can be fostered.

The great majority of manufacturers excel in building physical value into their products. Few excel in marketing "use value." This is the primary constraint on the accelerated growth of most businesses. Their markets, like all markets, are expert in perceiving value; that is what markets do all day. Yet manufacturers remain inexpert in marketing perceived value to them. This inequality of skill and the lack of common purpose between manufacturers and their markets account for a sizable number of new-product failures, short-lived brands, premature commodities, and mature commodities that fail to establish a branded repositioning.

Growth is completely dependent on premium profits. A growth strategy begins when we recognize that all profits initially reside in markets. Growing a business at an accelerated rate means capturing more of these profits faster. What kind of tradeoff can we offer a market in return? The answer is always the same: a preemptive perceived value or, in business terms, a branded benefit.

When we develop new products, we act as champions for the preemptive values that their markets must be able to perceive in them when they are commercialized. Technology venturing, discussed in Appendix C, is the best means of assuring new product competitiveness. When we enlarge the market penetration of new products, we act as translators of their preemptive value into the perceptions of the new market segments being penetrated. And when we restructure commodity products, we act as genetic engineers who splice preemptive value onto the perceptions of their traditional markets.

The value-to-price relationship of a brand may be expressed as follows: Premium value must always be perceived to be greater than premium price.

$$\text{Perceived Premium Value} > \text{Premium Price}$$
$$(\text{PPV}) > (\text{PP})$$

The premium value of a brand is its return, its yield, the incremental net worth that it confers on its user. Because this return comes about as a result of the investment made to acquire it, a brand's price is not a cost but an investment. A cost is a price that does not bear a positive return; an investment does.

The Concept of Perceived Value

When we define a brand's power as being derived from its *perceived value*, we are acknowledging the market genesis of branding. The perception of a product or a service as a brand originates in its market. While perceived value is sometimes directly correlated with manufactured or engineered value on a one-to-one basis, it often is not related to them. If we build a better mousetrap and that is all we do, it may not make any difference. Perceived value is based on value in use, not on value in the product. It is independent of the costs or technologies we put into a product.

Perceived value is dependent only on the benefits that can be derived from the product.

The test for perceived value is price. Markets pay for value. If high value is not perceived, a high price will not be paid. Price is therefore directly proportional to perceived value. The basis for premium price is what the market's perception of value will bear.

Recompetitive strategy is the process of building high values into markets. The physical product itself remains intact and unaffected. It is the marketing function that must add new and demonstrable market value. Perceptions of a market are to be engaged. This is the purpose of marketing: to create customer perceptions of preemptive value.

Ruling Out Debate on the Merits

Debate on the relative merits of competitive products is the bane of mature businesses. Ingredients, components, construction features, performance standards and operating benefits, deals and discounts, service, and even a product's bells, whistles, and flags are routinely opened for buyer scrutiny in the hope that some marginal advantage that can justify the maintenance of price will be discerned. Products that are feature-stripped and searched are, by definition, commodities. Brands are immune. How do brands rule out debate on the merits? The answer is straightforward: Brands are never marketed on the basis of their merits so they can never be compared according to them. Brands are marketed according to the values they add to their users, not the values that have been added to their products.

The Lincoln-Cadillac case illustrates brand power. For many years, Cadillac regularly outsold Lincoln by a margin of six or seven to one. Did this mean that Cadillac was six or seven times technically superior to Lincoln? Automotive experts have said that it was not. In fact, Lincoln was often superior in construction and performance. How, then, did Cadillac outsell Lincoln? Lincoln's analysis is short and sweet. "Lincoln added superior value to its car. Cadillac added superior value to the user."

So significant was this added user value that General Motors could say without effective challenge: "Cadillac is one of the few material possessions for which there is no true substitute." This reduced Lincoln to an untrue substitute, or a true nonsubstitute. The validation of Cadillac's claim to brandedness was the inexorable criterion of return on the user's investment: Cadillac owners received greater trade-in value for their cars than Lincoln owners. Given the tangible superiority in resale dollars for a Cadillac, how much incentive was there for buyers of American-made fine cars to debate the merits of construction and performance? The return on investment said it all. It was the embodiment of superior perceived value.

Merits, which is another way of saying values added to a product, are for hagglers to debate in the commodity bazaar. Brands rise above debate.

Passing the Acid Test

There is an acid test for branding. It answers the question, are we branded or not? The test is singular and unfailing. We are branded if we are the industry standard for delivering premier value to our customers. The premium value we deliver cannot be a product or service. It can only be growth: new profit dollars. This is the sole value for which customers will consistently pay us a premium price. In turn, the premium price they pay us will be the basis of our own growth. This is what recompetitiveness must accomplish. Either we are positioned as being branded or we are not positioned for growth. There is no other way to grow. Since no-growth or slow-growth is a recumbency and not an active posture, there is no other positioning.

To be positioned for growth, we must be positioned as the premier grower in our industry. Yet if we proclaim this position for ourselves, it will be self-serving and, therefore, self-defeating. Growers serve others, not themselves. Therefore, only the customers we grow can position us because they and they alone can testify credibly about our capability to grow them.

Branding is conferred on us by the customers we grow. This gives branding its authenticity. It also defines its rarity and explains why, like all things rare, it is so prized.

If we can become branded—that is, stamped with the imprint of a premier grower—we will hold in our hands the ultimate competitive weapon. Although our products and services may be equalized and their performance benefits reduced to parity by competitors, we need not lose our brand. Even worse, our products and services may be superseded, their performance benefits surpassed by competitors, and we can still maintain our brand. We may be the high-cost supplier and the high-price supplier, yet still hold on to our position as the branded supplier. As long as we can confer premier growth, our customers will confer branding and premier profits back upon us.

This is the essence of the brand concept. It circumvents the chancy and transient nature of product or service superiority of the moment as the basis for profitmaking. It says that product features and benefits are not the cause of branding; rather, branding is the effect they can have on customer growth. It makes price not a function of cost or "fair market value"—in other words, competitive price—but of customer value: how much customer growth is worth. Branded customers pay us for the value of their growth. We now have the same incentive they have; namely, to make them grow. For the first time, we and our customers can be partners and not adversaries.

Brand Pricing

The price of a brand has five characteristics:

1. Brand price is premium price.
2. Brand price is compared with the improved profit the brand contributes to a customer's business, not to competitive prices.
3. Brand price is recoverable by the customer's improved profit, eliminating price as a purchase decision.

4. Brand price is not negotiable.
5. Brand price varies in direct proportion to each customer's improved profit. Improved customer profit is the brand's "product." Since no two customers are the same, no two branded products can be the same. Therefore, brand price is always customer-specific.

These characteristics show how different brand pricing is from vendor pricing. This is because the effect of branding is to rule out price as the basis for purchase—and price is the only basis that exists for commodity selling. Since a brand's purpose is to add value to its user, not to add a product to the user's inventory, brand price is attached to that value. It bears some proportion to its worth. The financial worth of the physical product or service is irrelevant. Its performance helps the customer achieve his added value, but it does not do so alone. Brand price is not pinned solely to the product. Instead, it is the consequence of the customer's total benefit.

Customer-Driven Pricing

Price is not the cause of customer value; it is the result. Commodity selling makes price the cause. Low price is positioned as creating customer value by lowering acquisition cost. Brand pricing turns things around. The customers' value is the financial value added by the brander. This value causes the price, which is positioned as the result of the customers' incremental worth.

Branding makes pricing customer-driven. It does not ask customers what price they would like to pay or if they think a certain price is fair. It asks what new value they need to receive and what investment they are willing to make to obtain it. Brand price gives evidence of what a benefit is worth to the customers who will be rewarded by it. It is not what we think it ought to be. It is what the customers think it is, based on their valuation of a dollar's worth at the point in time when they do business with us.

By knowing how much value we stand for, we can measure

our worth as an investment. We will know how good an option we are as a repository for our customers' discretionary funds. The higher our rate of return and the sooner it accrues, the better investment we will be. This is the "product" we will install in our customers' businesses, what we will put to work for them, and what will improve their profits. When it is a good product—when its dollar-for-dollar performance is high—we can sell it with confidence and pride.

The value-basing of price forces us to know the value on which price will be based. Where can we look to find the value? It will always be in the life-style or work-style of our customers. We do not make value. Only our customers can make value. It comes out of the way they apply our products and services in their operations, their functions, and their processes. Value is performance value: value in use, not measurable at the point of manufacture or the point of sale, but at the point of application and implementation.

Asking Brand Questions

The single most crucial component of brand strategy is determining a brand's value-based price point. It will almost always be higher than we first dare. This is because we are limited in our knowledge. We know a brand's cost; only its users know its value and therefore what they will pay to gain it.

We can now see clearly the three questions of utmost significance that we must ask of each potential brand that we conceive:

1. *Who is its market?* Who will have value added to them?
2. *What value will they receive?* How much added value will they benefit from?
3. *How much will it be worth to them?* What will they invest to achieve the value?

The answer to the third question tells us the price. It comes from the answer to the second question, which tells us the basis for price. The area of knowledge represented by the second question is the brander's stock in trade. To know the value that we bring to our customers and not just the cost we represent is the database for brand price. To be a brander means to be a value-bringer. It is not enough to know we bring a value. Nor is it enough to know the nature of the value we bring. We must also know *how much.*

II
CONCENTRATE

2

Niche the Market

Recompetitiveness is a market-narrowing process. It is a reversal of the endless search a mature business makes for volume, a search that broadens and deepens its market. In order to keep unit costs as low as possible and to make up in quantity what is lost in margins, maturity forces every potential customer to be sought out and sold. No one must get away. A 90 percent share of market today demands a 91 percent share tomorrow. Most mature companies like to say they will not stop sharebuilding until they have 100 percent of their market. Some, with a nod to the spirit of competition, settle—at least publicly—for a mere 99 percent.

Broad, deep markets are costly markets. The Pareto Principle tells us that fewer than 20 percent of all customers, no matter how many there are, will account for more than 80 percent of profits. These are core customers, the heavy profit contributors. They may or may not be high-volume customers. But they constitute "the market" as far as profits from sales are concerned.

The remaining 80 percent or so of all customers yields as little as 20 percent or less of all profits. To make matters worse, they are the source of a disproportionate amount of costs. They are costly to identify. They are costly to convert. They are costly to serve. They are costly to maintain. Yet maturity leaves no choice. We must sell something to everybody. The need for incremental revenue outranks its incremental cost. The asset base must be recapitalized again and again. That requires cash and not profits. To obtain it, we must always improve productivity. Notably, we must sell harder.

Hodgepodging versus Eighty-Twentying

Mature markets are a hodgepodge. They contain heavy users and light users mixed in with heavy profit contributors and light profit contributors. Many heavy users are light profit contributors because they buy on price. In contrast, there are light users who are heavy profit contributors because they buy on value. There are customers who could be divested without loss. Others who cost more to serve than they return could be divested at a gain. And there are customers whose loss would be irreparable because they are the basic source of profits.

Hodgepodge markets are an unaffordable liability. They, and the volume-based business that supplies them, must be downsized for restructuring. Otherwise, the costs of marketing volume—inventorying it, warehousing it, distributing it, selling it, collecting on it—will overwhelm the profits. Instead of "something for everybody," the basic marketing principle of competitive maturity must be "something for somebody" or "everything for somebody." But the concept of *everybody* must go. Growth after maturity is the result of progressive market narrowing.

Market narrowing begins with the 20 percent of customers who are currently contributing up to 80 percent of our profits from sales. These will be the base of our recompetitive business. They assure it a high rate of per-unit profit. They have already discovered their ability to benefit significantly from doing business with us. In many cases, they have quantified our added value, compared it with our price, and classified us as a bargain—as a source of value that is greater than its cost. They are content to buy on the value they recieve. Price loses its discriminatory role. Our margins are accepted.

Our 20 percent customers who pay premium margins are

telling us something: We are growing them. The values we are adding to their profits, either by reducing their operating costs or increasing their productivity or sales revenues, are accelerating their growth. They are willing to pay us for the value of the new profits we are supplying. We may think of our transactions as "selling our product." Core customers know better. They think of us as improving their profits.

If customers are doing business with us to improve their profits, they will calculate the costs and benefits of their relationship with us. They will know the excess of their benefits over our cost; this will be their definition of margin. Unless we understand that this is how they buy, we will never know the true value of the benefits we provide. Our focus will be fixed on the investment we are making to generate the revenues we receive from them. These, however, are *our own costs* and benefits, not those of our customers. Ignorance of what we are really selling leads directly to our inability to price it fully. Poverty of customer knowledge ensures poverty of supplier profits.

The first commandment for restructuring our competitiveness is to do everything we can to maintain our business with customers whose growth we are already improving. Over the long run, the only way to maintain it will be to enhance it. The second commandment for restructuring is to search out and serve additional customers we are not currently growing but whose businesses we are equally able to grow. Taken together, these two customer groups form our *growth niche*.

Every business that restructures must turn first to niching its market. Retailing, one of the oldest industries, has been de-departmentalizing its stores, getting out of general merchandise, and restructuring its outlets into specialty stores-within-the-store or free-standing self-contained specialty centers that serve specific niche customers.

Carson Pirie Scott operates three stores-within-the-store. One specializes in the youth niche, another in the homemaker niche, and a third in the business executive niche. Montgomery Ward has converted its general merchandise stores into self-contained specialty stores that serve the home and automotive markets. Sears has organized a separate chain of Business Systems Centers that sell computers. K mart operates specialty home centers and a separate chain of drug retailers. Warehouse-type specialty stores are located all over the country, catering to the home improvement market niche or home electronics customers.

In every case, the specialty stores are more customer-sensitive and, as their reward, more profitable. Because they are exclusively driven by their market niches, they can flexibly respond to changes in customer tastes for styles or fashions and even anticipate them at times. Their return on equity shows the result. It averages almost 30 percent, double the 15 percent traditional average for the top department store companies.

Retailers' catalogs are also becoming niched. Sears has two dozen "Specialogs," each focused on a specific market: power tools, toys, petite clothing, and so forth. Spiegel publishes more than 30 different catalogs. Montgomery Ward, on the other hand, has gone out of the catalog business after 113 years. It refused to niche its general catalog.

Competitive maturity begins with one market-narrowing question: *Who can we grow?* The answer will be the customer niche that will, in turn, give us the growth that will make us competitive. They will be the customers who are, right now, paying unnecessary direct costs to run operations in their major business functions where we are process-smart. Or they will be the customers who are, right now, paying the unnecessary opportunity costs of unrealized sales in their major markets where we are also process-smart or sales-smart. No others need apply.

Two-Tier Segmentation

Growing and growable customers make up a market whose narrowness seems exaggeratedly small when it is compared against a mature company's traditional mass market. Because it is profit-based rather than volume-based, it represents only 20 percent or so of the total market. Even though it accounts for up to 80 percent of profits, it may appear to be a fragile foundation for the growth of an asset-heavy business. What about the other 80 percent of the market? What should be done about it?

The 80-20 rule operates whether we recognize it or not. Every mature business is already deriving the majority of its profits from a minority of its customers. In most cases, though, there are no obvious signs that this is so. Heavy volume users, not heavy profit contributors, are worshipped. They get the special attention. Even if they are neither being grown nor are growable, they are given the same attention as customers who can be grown. This is because only their purchasing needs are sold to; their needs for improved profits go unattended.

All profits are not created equal. Some profits are far more cost-effectively earned, and therefore possess higher quality, than others. Nor are all customers equal in their ability to create profits for us. To be competitive in maturity demands that the monolithic concept of a universal market composed of equal customers be divided into a two-tier segmentation. Segment one, the narrow top tier, will be composed of growing and growable customers. They will be the source of our mature competitiveness. The second segment, the bottom tier, will be all the others, the 80 percent that will contribute the remaining 20 percent of the profits. These will be our two markets. The top tier will grow us. We must dedicate ourselves to it. The bottom tier will challenge our ability to sell to it in the most cost-effective manner. How low can we make our cost of sales? How effectively can we manage each customer relationship at that cost so that we maximize our earnings at minimal expenditure?

Our top-tier business will be our "branded" business. It will make us competitive. Our bottom-tier business will remain a commodity business. It will supplement our earnings. It will not be our growth source, nor will we be a growth source for its customers.

The market universe of a competitive mature business can be visualized as a pyramid. As Figure 2-1 shows, the top tier is the niche market—the 20 percent of all customers who will make our business competitive. While small in size, it possesses a disproportionate power to grow us. The larger portion of the pyramid contains our slow-growth and no-growth market. Large in size

Figure 2-1. The two-tier market pyramid.

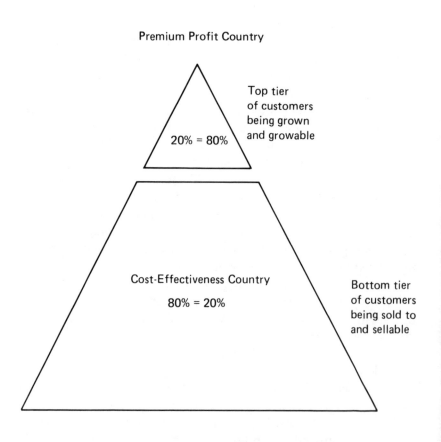

Premium Profit Country

Top tier
of customers
being grown
and growable

20% = 80%

Cost-Effectiveness Country

80% = 20%

Bottom tier
of customers
being sold to
and sellable

but powerless to drive our growth, it will ensure perpetual mature status for us if it remains the focus of our business strategy.

The line of least resistance for the typical mature business is to go on doing what it has been doing but to do it a little bit better. This means it will concentrate on two strategies. It will reduce its costs, especially manufacturing expenses that will enable it to be a low-cost producer when measured against competition. At the same time, it will seek to increase its volume to become a market share leader. In both of these strategies, competition is the driving force. This is the hallmark of maturity: competitors, not customers, drive decisions.

As a result, maturity prejudices our insights. We look inward to our own businesses where we preoccupy ourselves with our costs. Similarly, we try to look inward to the businesses of our competitors to decipher their costs so we can compare them with our own. Cost reduction becomes our central strategy. Productivity improvement is one way to achieve it. Buying on price from low bidders is another. Volume production and sales is the third.

Where is the customers' role? They are our afterthought. We look outward to seek them and to sell and serve them only when we have implemented the cost reduction strategies imposed on us by the drive force of competition. By then, we run headlong into the cost reduction strategies of our customers. Most of what we know about them comes out of this confrontational relationship. We say they are price-sensitive. We see them as cost-conscious, penny-pinching and tight-fisted. We know everything about how they save money and hardly anything about how they grow it. Our sales process becomes a process of cost justification. Marketing means being sure we get requests for proposals and bidding low on them.

The Volume Trap

Volume is not the key to profits. High unit margins—premium prices—are the multiplicand of profits. Volume is their multiplier. A growth business has both. An increasing volume multiplies the profitmaking capability of high unit margins. It is at maturity, when unit margins have become depressed, that attention becomes fixated on their multiplier. Since the margins cannot be raised on each unit, the number of units must be raised if profits are to grow. As margins shrink further, the burden of ever-increasing volume becomes more and more oppressive. Volume seems the apparent salvation. In reality, it is a profit trap.

Mature businesses embrace volume in many ways. To assure quantity purchases, they give away price in the form of deals, discounts, and rebates. They also enter into exclusive-supplier agreements where they trade off margins for the cost-lowering continuity of manufacturing and sales. When they become a sole supplier, they proclaim in falsely based exhilaration that "we have the customer sewed up." In reality, it may be the customer who has tied them hand and foot to a long-term lowball price that guarantees commodity margins with no power to grow. Sales will swell, the costs of manufacture and sales may subside, but commensurate profits will be absent.

Volume is not contrary to profits. But it is not directly proportional to them either. Unless our heavy-using customers pay full margins or buy at a premium price above them, they may be part of the 80 percent of customers that deliver only 20 percent of profits. It may appear that "they are keeping us alive" because the cash flow pays the rent. Staying alive and growing, however, are two different things.

The 20 percent of customers who hold our growth in their hands are always our heavy profit sources. Sometimes they are also our heavy volume users. Far more often than not, the rank order of the profit-twenty will be different from the rank order of the volume-twenty. This tells us something about growth. Volume customers typically support our commodity business. They help bring down our unit costs. They take advantage of it by bringing down our unit margins. Because they themselves are usually mature businesses, as testified by the size of the orders they place, they are highly price-sensitive and cost-constrained. Their growth is more likely to be accomplished by cost reduction than by sales revenue increases. They already control a sizable market share, which they cannot cost-effectively enlarge. Or they are in an oligopolistic industry where sales revenues cannot be permanently gained but can only be traded among the oligarchs.

Growth is more predictably represented to us by smaller, faster evolving business for whom market penetration and market sharebuilding are urgent. They will be consistent purchasers. They will pay high margins because of the high value we can offer them: the enhancement of their ability to sell at high margins. They, not the mature volume buyers, are our prime "growables." They are already growing. Furthermore, they are dedicated to continue growth at a superior rate.

Our Game

The market of growables is the market niche where we are good at growing customers. It is the arena of our greatest expertise; it is "our game." If we cannot grow at playing our game—doing what we are best at—we cannot grow at all. The art of regaining competitiveness at maturity is to return to our premier skills. In the process, we will learn how far we have strayed from them in trying to sell something to everybody.

Who we can grow is predetermined by what we are good at. But that puts the cart before the horse. If we are to be genuinely market-driven, what we are good at should be predetermined by who we can grow. Narrowing the market to our most likely growth customers is the first step. It is the cause of growth.

If we are data processing systems suppliers, our game is improving customer profits by applying data processing technology to some of their business functions. When we apply our technology to inventory control and warehousing functions, for example, we can reduce their costs. When we apply our technology to credit and collection functions, we can increase their revenues. These are the ways in which we grow our customers. Our most growable customers will be businesses that depend heavily on the functions we can improve—namely, large multiproduct manufacturers.

Other than organizations like IBM, AT&T, and "Japan Inc.," which are fully integrated suppliers, data processing manufacturers have all had to find their game and, along with it, their niche:

Company	*Niche*
NCR	Retailing
Control Data	Science and Engineering
Honeywell	Process control
Burroughs	Hospitals
Sperry	Government
Qantel	Professional football and basketball

If we are health care system suppliers, our game is improving customer profits by applying health care technology to some of their business functions. When we apply our technology to laboratory functions, we can reduce their costs. When we apply our technology to staff training functions, we can increase their productivity. These are the ways in which we grow our customers. Our most growable customers will be businesses that depend heavily on the functions we can improve: medium and large hospitals and health maintenance organizations.

If we are building materials system suppliers, our game is improving customer profits by applying building construction technology to some of their business functions. When we apply our technology to materials handling functions, we can reduce their costs. When we apply our technology to roof-building functions, we can increase their revenues by accelerating the inflow of rental income. These are the ways in which we grow our customers. Our most growable customers will be businesses that depend heavily on the functions we can improve: large commercial building contractors.

In each case, we have assumed two things. One is that we possess a dual capability for growing customers. We can grow them by reducing their costs, or we can grow them by increasing their revenue-producing capacity. In reality, this may not always be true; we may be able to grow customers in only one of these two ways. The second assumption we have made is that our customers can be grown in both of these two ways. This may not always be true either.

Mature suppliers are the result of mature customers. If our customers are in a stable mode without growth or if they are in a negative growth mode, cost reduction will be paramount. Every cost advantage must be pursued. Unless we can help them increase their sales to their own growable customers, we may not be able to increase our own sales to them. We may be reduced to being partial growers. This is better than not growing them—and ourselves—at all. But to grow fully up to our capability, we will have to find customers whose sales revenues we can grow. These will be customers who are themselves growing because their customers are growing.

To a growing customer, sales revenues and market share, not cost reduction, are paramount. Customers we can help grow by further helping them increase profitable sales revenues are the *sine qua non* of growth. Without them, we can become quasicompetitive at maturity. But our competitiveness will be limited by the same constraints that imprison our mature customers. They, and us along with them, will be constricted in growth by mature markets.

The lesson we must learn is that, to play our game, we may have to move away from our traditional customer base if it cannot be grown by increased sales to its own customers. We will have to seek out growth customers. These may be smaller, more entrepreneurial businesses than we are accustomed to serving. They will be on a growth curve whose demands can be different, in the frenzy of their pace and in their quality, from those we are accustomed to coping with. They may even be businesses in a different market, businesses with different cost structures and different customers of their own. Yet if we want to become competitive at maturity, we may be forced to reniche our top-tier market. The alternative is stark: for us and our mature markets to decline, decay, and divest in noncompetitive concert.

III

CHAMPION

3

Team the Growers

Making a business recompetitive is a shared process. No single
function of a business can accomplish it alone. A business as a
whole cannot even regain competitiveness by itself. Two types of
partnering must take place. One type teams two internal functions, profit center management and sales management. The second type partners them with similar teams in the customer
businesses that compose our niche market.

Internal teaming creates a new organization unit, the growth
team. The team's objective is to drive competitive growth. Its
driver's mission is to grow the customer partners by reducing their
cost problems and expanding their sales opportunities.

A model growth team and its customer counterpart are
shown in Figures 3-1 and 3-2. They are the champions that will
make mature growth their cause. The supplier team grows the
customer team. The customer team grows the supplier team. Both
businesses may be mature. Each may make and market undiffer-
entiated, parity commodity products. Neither may possess a marketing or technological advantage. Yet each team will be able to
grow the other.

Each growth team is a microcosm of its total corporate
power. Like a lens, it focuses the amorphous corporate strength
on specific targets: a specific cost to be reduced by a specific

Figure 3-1. Growth team.

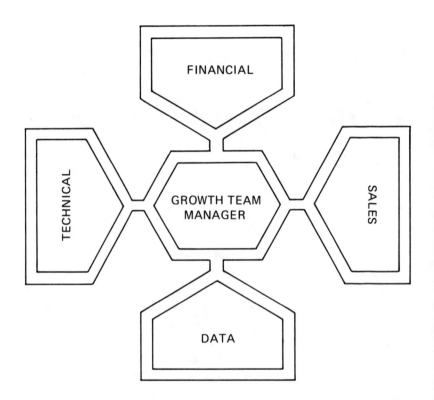

amount in a specific customer business function; or a specific
amount of increased revenues to be gained by a specific customer
line of business. When we combine internal capabilities that are
ordinarily only loosely related and concentrate them on selected
objectives, growth becomes congenial. If there is a secret to competitive maturity, it is in the one-to-one alliance of dedicated
growth teams with their customer growth teams.

Growth teams are an attempt to imbed entrepreneur management into a mature business without disorganizing or reorganiz-
ing the business. Nor must the cherished concept of its culture be
confronted. Only a relatively small number of people will be affected. But they are the key drivers of competitiveness.

Figure 3-2. Customer growth team.

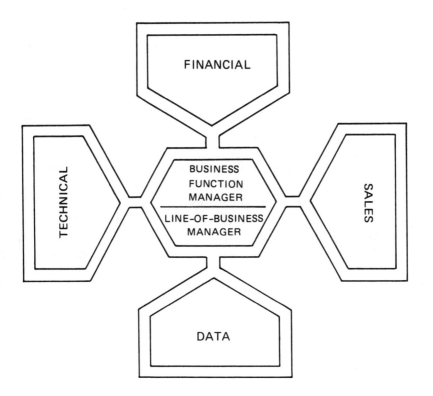

The Entrepreneur Capability

Because customers must be grown first before a mature business can become competitive, the composition of a growth team is self-determining. A data manager is needed to validate where customers can be grown. This is the team's "where-man." Sales and technical managers are needed to apply a product to customer operations so that it will grow their ability to profit. They are the team's "how-men." A financial manager is needed to quantify the amount and rate of new profit contribution. This is the team's "how-much-man." The driver who coordinates them, who leads and manages the team, is its "who-man." This is the paramount responsibility. The driver selects customers who are the most likely growables. If the driver is wrong, maturity will persist and competitiveness will be denied.

This is the minimal team. All other resources can be drawn from the corporate asset base on a pro-tem basis as they are required, using the asset base for what it is—a mighty reservoir of talent and funds. External resources, usually of a specialized nature, can also be allied to the growth team when corporate staffs are neither adequate nor available.

Growth teams operate with simple charters. A team's objective is to grow one or more top-tier customers who will grow the team's profits in return. A team is evaluated by the customers it grows: how much growth it provides, at what rate, how dependably, and with what continuity. Since team growth is the reciprocal of customer growth, a growth team will be able to grow its own business in direct proportion to the rate, the amount, the dependability, and the continuity with which it grows its customers.

Entrepreneur Model Building

Mature organizations are self-perpetuating. They breed maturity. The sole role models for mature-business managers are other mature-business managers. Because culture predicts strategy, each year reflects the past year more than the next year. Plans continue to be made and measured by the pound rather than by—and with—the customer. Innovation comes to mean a new size for a product, a new shape, or a new performance rating: something novel to its makers but not to its market.

In the milieu of maturity, a growth team offers a fresh perspective. Familiar people are doing unfamiliar things. Managers, made more entrepreneurial, exude a different style and substance. They can streamline their decisionmaking process, avoiding corporate drag. Their responsibility is clear-cut: improve profits or take the consequences. As a result, they have a greater role in determining their strategic options and acting on them than their counterparts in the corporate bureaucracy.

A growth team is a living laboratory. Its entrepreneur management style, its growth planning process, its customer-partnering mode of doing business and its profit improvement strategies for consumating partnerships are a showcase for the organization as a whole. Other managers of mature businesses can study the team's leadership, organization, and operations. They can apply some or all of them selectively, even to a business that is not yet ready to become newly competitive but is in a state of anticipation. This can give them a head start. Or it may provide the incentive for a manger who is on the fence to come forward and declare for competitive growth.

Nothing proves that mature businesses can regain growth like an in-house model of a mature business—one of "our very own"—that is newly growing. This makes competitive maturity a part of the Invented Here Syndrome. By the mere fact of its existence down the hall, it provokes belief and incites imitation.

A living, working model also serves an additional purpose. A genuine growth manager is available on premises for counsel, providing internal consultation services to managers who want to grow and who need to find out firsthand what it is like.

In these ways, both by training and practice as well as by inspiration, growth teams build growers. The new profit dollars that growth represents are the immediate result of teaming growers. But the growers themselves, trained in entrepreneur management strategies and style, are the more enduring result. As long as growth strategies remain in place, whatever is invested to train growers will yield a greater return than 80 percent of the business lines in a mature company as a whole.

This is the value added by entrepreneur management. A good growth team models entrepreneur strategies for the rest of its organization. It attracts entrepreneurs, retains them, educates them in fast-growth management, and recycles them into successive growth opportunities. Growth teams provide a showcase to study growth managers: how they grow, how they strategize, what they emphasize and what they ignore, how they maximize time, and how they achieve market and industry dominance.

Driver Standards Of Performance

The drivers' standards of performance are unique to the growth teams. Drivers perform five keystone strategies:
    1. *Profit Maximization.* Drivers set the dual profit objectives for the growth team. First they set the customer's profit improvement objectives. Then they set their own team's profit improvement objectives. This two-pronged emphasis on profit provides the team's entrepreneurial thrust. To implement it, they must pursue four additional strategies.
    2. *Marketing Leverage.* Drivers must act as guardians of the product. Their principal task is to make sure that it is left alone. Unless it is significantly deficient in the customer's perceptions, drivers must resist the temptation to renovate it. Instead, they must manage growth leverage through marketing strategies rather than technology.
    3. *Minimal Strategies.* Drivers must keep their marketing strategy mix to a minimum. They must select the smallest number of strategies to apply against each growth customer that will ensure the maximum improvement of customer profits. There are two compelling reasons to minimize the team's strategy mix. One is to permit cost-effectiveness by keeping the cost base down. The other is to permit the growth team to concentrate on applying a small system of strategies exceedingly well. Each strategy can then make its full contribution to customer growth.
    4. *Product Branding.* Drivers differentiate their offerings from all others by supplying the most beneficial new profit. The improved profit they sell can be differentiated by its amount, its rate, or its dependability, or any combination. This brands their product. Branding gives drivers the right to command a premium price in return for premium value.
    5. *Market Dominance.* Drivers must make their team's ability to improve customer profits the dominant source of growth in their customer markets. The team must create the industry standards for customer growth. The profits that can be improved by customer cost reduction must become their customer industry's standard cost reduction. Similarly, the profits that can be im-

proved by customer revenue increases must become their customer industry's standard revenue increase. Any rival teams who go up against these standards must fall short in amount, rate, or dependability.

The role of growth drivers may be summarized this way: They fulfill their standards of performance best when they keep the product from being renovated and the strategy mix from being enlarged beyond its minimum; at the same time, they leverage marketing to penetrate customer growth opportunity, brand their offering to merit premium price, and position themselves and their team as the dominant source of profit supply for their industry. As a result, they are able to maximize the profits they contribute to their customers and to their own company.

Teach-Learn Partnerships

A growth team is a collective partnership among the driver and the other teammates. They must share the twin objectives of growing their customers and thereby growing themselves. That is their joint responsibility. They must also share in the rewards. A team bonus based on incremental profits or a profit share are common incentives. Since each member benefits only when the team as a whole benefits, the team can present a unified front to its customer correlates when it offers itself in partnership with them.

By itself, a growth team represents one half of a partnership. It needs a customer team in order to function. It must therefore take the initiative in teaching customers how to organize their teams and how to integrate them in a mutually beneficial partnership for profits. This is a team's initial sales challenge. It does not have to ask a customer to buy anything. Instead, it should teach the profit-improvement advantages of one-to-one growth teaming. When a customer accepts the invitation to organize its own growth team, that customer is implicitly accepting partnering.

The act of teaching the advantages of growth teaming is the first lesson in the growth curriculum. A growth team is essentially a teaching organization. It teaches customers how to improve their profits. Drawing on its general expertise in reducing the cost contribution of customer business functions and increasing the revenue contribution from customer markets, a growth team takes an educational position with its customers. You are managing certain functions in an unnecessarily costly manner, the team says; we have expertise in reducing these costs. Or the team will say, You are unnecessarily underselling certain markets; we have expertise in raising these sales.

The growth team's function is to allow its customers to learn by doing. In order to conduct learning as partners, a customer's learning and doing must be in concert with the growth team. Both partners can then learn together. The customer learns profit improvement through more cost-effective operations and sales management. The growth team learns how to improve customer profits even more. Since costs can always be reduced and sales revenues can always be increased, the partnership's work will never be done.

Recompetitiveness can be said to begin when a customer perceives a supplier growth team as a source of its growth. This means that the team is no longer positioned as a source of products, services, or systems. It is no longer an alternate vendor. Its business is to supply improved profits on a partnered basis. The relationship between a growth team and its customers is not predicated on buying and selling commodity products on a price-performance basis. Instead, it is a financial relationship. The customer places a premium investment with the team. This grows the team. The team transforms these investments into a premium rate of return that grows the customer.

Growth teams sell money, not products. They transact returns from investments, not sales. Their price is an investment, not a cost. Their performance is measured by the amount and rate of the customer's return, not product performance benefits. They work inside their customer businesses as partners, not from the outside as vendors. They relate directly to customer business function managers and profit center managers, not purchasing agents. They work at these middle management levels on a long-term, continuing basis, not from bid to bid. Their focus is not on competitive suppliers but on competitive profitmaking for their customer partners and for themselves.

The best definition of growth teams is that they are customer growers. They go right to the source of growth, middle customer managers who control business function costs and center their company's profitmaking responsibilities. They propose growth to these decisionmakers, quantifying it in dollar terms of net profit and in percentage terms of rate of return on investment.

Both partners will become more proficient over time. Together, they will learn how each of them can earn greater growth profits by working together. This knowledge will reside in the heads of the members of the two growth teams. It will also be the stuff of which the teams' joint database is made. The database will provide the historical record of what happens when the growth team applies its expertise and its capabilities to the customer's business. These records will become the partnership's norms. The database will also contain the priority rank ordering of as-yet unsolved customer problems and unrealized customer opportunities for future resolution.

Joint Growth Planning

Mature businesses plan alone. They plan in secret, in proprietary privacy lest competitors gain foreknowledge of this year's strategies for infringing on rival shares of market. If the truth were known, their competitors' plans are virtual replicas of their own. Except for the names, the plans of most mature businesses could be exchanged with one another without adding significantly to their competitive intelligence or altering very much about their strategies.

The bane of maturity is to plan against competition instead of planning, as growth businesses plan, to grow their customers. Mature plans are obsessed with their competitive strengths and weaknesses. They itemize whose market shares they will conquer and by how much. They stockpile contingencies against competitive strategies that have a low probability of taking place but are perceived to be a major threat precisely for that very reason. Meanwhile, the customer is segmented into price-based classifications but otherwise ignored.

When growth is the transcendent objective, planning alone becomes an anachronism. Since growth depends on customer growth, it is unthinkable to suppose that customers can be planned *for*. Customers can only be planned *with*. It is their growth that we must accelerate; their growth that we must integrate with; their shares of market that we must help expand; their competitors that we must help them anticipate and overcome. For these reasons, planning between growers must be joint.

The product of joint planning is a joint growth plan—mutual growth objectives and the strategy mix to achieve them that is prepared, implemented, and controlled in concert by the planners.

Each growth team has the same role in the joint planning process. It is to answer the question, How can the customer partner best be grown? The customer's growth team will set the plan's customer objectives. How much growth is required? How much growth must come from cost reduction or increased productivity—by what business functions? How much growth must come from increased sales revenues—from what lines of business sold to which markets?

At this point, the supplier growth team can go to work. Here is the contribution we can make to cost reduction or productivity: Here are the business functions we can affect, here are the costs we can decrease, here are the profits we can save. Here is the contribution we can make to increased sales revenues: Here are the markets we can affect, here are the lines of business whose sales we can increase, here are the profits we can add. In both costs and sales revenues, here are some other things we can also do and here are the incremental profits they can earn. For the year as a whole, here are the new profit dollars you can expect from our growth partnership over the next 12 months. Is this a significant contribution? If not, what will be?

The plan that emerges is not "our plan" or "their plan" but a joint plan.

It is obvious that the act of implementing a jointly prepared plan can unite the partners who install it. Less obvious but equally binding, the act of preparing a joint plan can partner the growth teams as co-conspirators in mutual profit enhancement. Would-be third partners have no operating base because they have no planning base. They can still sell as vendors. But the high-margin, big-winner sales will already have been planned for.

IV
CUSTOMIZE

4

Displace the Product

Recompetitiveness reveals the difference between beefing up a product and weighing it down. As a product becomes mature, it puts on the weight of its asset base that, up until then, had been beefing it up. But with age, the costs inherent in the asset base emerge. They redefine assets in terms of *costs,* whereas we had previously thought of our assets only in terms of their *capabilities.* Now we know them for what they are. As costs, they must be met. Not only met, they must be exceeded. As it becomes more and more difficult to do this, they consume more and more of our thinking. Insidiously, they take over the business and begin to drive it.

Maturity is homecoming for a product's costs. Once a product is cost-driven, a role reversal occurs between manufacturing and marketing. Manufacturing becomes the master; marketing is its slave. The capacity to produce takes over as the determinant of volume rather than the capacity to sell at high margins. Learning curve economics, not profits, dominate the business. Lowest unit costs transcend highest unit margins as the supreme business objective.

These facts set up the moment in time that can be called the undeniable "realization of maturity." It occurs when an additional dollar invested in a product's asset base will no longer return a competitive yield. The return may fail to be competitive with the hurdle rate for new products. Or it may be lower than competitive investments are offering for the same dollar, even lower than the rate of return from other mature businesses.

This is the product's point of no return.

It is at this point that managers typically turn to their product to see how they can enhance its appeal. Invariably, they work from two objectives. One is to enable the product to perform superior benefits for its current market. The other is to enable the product to perform more benefits that will broaden its market to include new users. Both these objectives guarantee failure. At maturity, a product should become specialized rather than more generalized. And unless it is significantly deficient, it should not be enhanced at all.

A universal law governs the futility of product enhancement. Products are devalued by maturity. As their performance loses its differentiation, price becomes the exclusive variable that can be made distinctive. This is the reason for price manipulation: It offers a point of distinction. All things are equal in maturity except price. The purchase decision will therefore almost always be made on price. If product enhancement could convey performance superiority so that all things were not equal, price would also become superior. But mature enhancement can accomplish only two results. First, the product's asset base will be increased, adding to its cost. Second, breakeven will be elevated, costs of manufacture will be increased, and sales costs will also rise. By the time a new value-price-cost relationship can be consolidated, competition will replicate the enhancement at a lower cost. A commodity product business will still be a commodity product business. Only the entry fee will be raised, not the margins.

Maturity requires us to stop selling a product as a product. Its productness must be displaced in favor of something that can be differentiated and therefore can be sold at a premium price. What offering should displace the product? What must the new "product" be?

Figures 4-1 and 4-2 represent the before and after of the product displacement process. In Figure 4-1, the product is the star. Price is attached to it. Product-related services, inventory

Figure 4-1. Product-starred system.

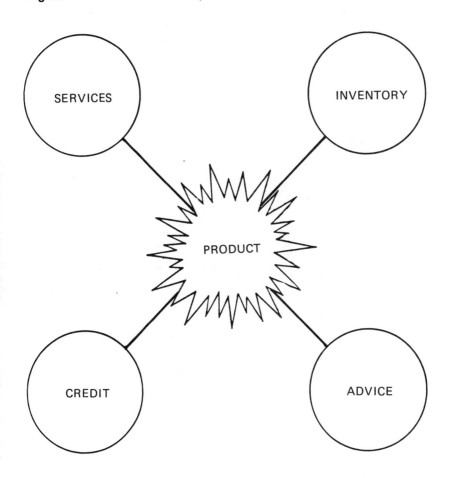

control for customers, credit extension, and implementation advice are all provided free as added values to sweeten the product. Each is a hidden price offer. At the same time that they add value to the product, they devalue its margins. Competitors can equal them without delay.

In Figure 4-2, the product has been displaced by customer profits as the new "product." Profits are now the star. The physical product, along with its related services, credit extension, and implementation advice, is one of several component values that

Figure 4-2. Profit-starred system.

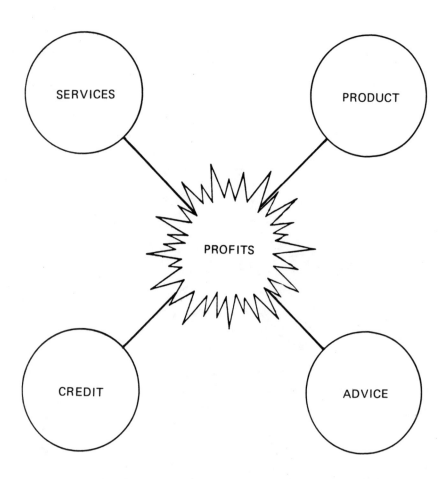

contribute to customer profits. Price has been removed from the product. It is attached to the total value of customer profits that the system as a whole, including the product, can contribute. A new star has been born. Along with it, so has competitive maturity.

Once it has given up differentiation, a starred product announces a commodity business. "Price selling," it might just as well say, "is spoken here." On the other hand, a business makes a very different statement about itself when it stars customer profits: "Customer growth spoken here." This is the language of mutual profit improvement.

The Concept of "Enoughness"

Mature products are rarely technologically inferior to competition. Mostly they are at parity. If they suffer from inferiority, it is insignificant. The performance values they offer are standard, not substandard. Even in unusual cases where a product's performance is technically deficient, this is not a compelling reason to deter its restructuring into a more competitive maturity.

In order for a product to become recompetitive, it is not necessary to enhance its performance to the point of superiority. All it must achieve is "enoughness"—the ability to deliver an optimal benefit rather than the maximum benefit.

The optimal benefit lies at the intersection of minimal value and the maximum price that can be obtained for the minimal value. We can define minimal value as sufficient value—enough value to enable the product to perform sufficiently well so that it can make a significant contribution to improving customer profit. This means it must be *good enough* to do what it has to do, no better and no worse. As long as a mature product is good enough, we must not enhance it.

If we embark on a "search for excellence" to maximize a product's value, we set forth on a fool's errand. We will overdesign, overengineer, and overcost, and as a result, we will be forced to overprice. We will move toward the theoretical solution that, even if it were achievable, few customers would buy; few customers need maximum performance or are willing and able to pay for it. Excellence, or maximum performance, is both unaffordable by our customers and unmarketable by us.

Maximum performance is a technical concept. We should leave it in the laboratory where it belongs. Optimal performance is a market's concept. It originates with our customers, growing out of the amount of profit they need to have improved. We must learn it from them and apply it to our business. This is the essence of being market-driven. How little profit improvement will you regard as significant? We must ask our markets. How *little* cost do you need to have reduced? How *few* new sales dollars do you need to have increased? The answers will define "enoughness" for our product. If we underachieve it, we will offer less effectiveness than our price justifies. This is the minor likelihood. If we over-achieve it, we will offer more effectiveness than our price can recover because it is more effectiveness than our market values.

Every dollar invested in performance enhancement must eventually be paid back by price. The smaller the investment, the lower will be the cost base of price and the higher its realized margin can be. Dollars invested to exceed "enoughness" allocate resources without the promise of payback. They waste money. Even worse, they waste the unrecoverable time of development people. This is our scarcest and most transient resource. The opportunity cost of their misallocation is our true penalty for exceeding "enoughness." What else, we must always ask ourselves, could they have been doing in that same time that would give us a greater payoff?

Our ego drive to produce the best product and our market's drive to produce the best profits are incompatible. It is not our best products, even if we can manufacture and market them at a profit to ourselves, that will provide the growth of our customers that will make us competitive. It is how skillfully we can *apply* them to improve customer profits that will improve our own growth. This requires maximizing customer profits, not maximizing product performance.

Product Rebranding Strategy

When customer profits can once again be maximized, we can say that we have been successful in *rebranding* our product—that is, in giving it back the command of premium price. Rebranding is a four-step process. In its course, the product is first systemized. Then the financial impact of the system is sold. The selling price of the system is based on its ability to improve customer profits, not on its components. Finally, the system is made available through financing so that customer capital can be conserved, enhancing still further the amount of profits that can be improved.

1. Systemize the Product

A mature product cannot stand alone. Naked to the world, it will soon find its margins have been picked clean. It must be protected from margin erosion by surrounding it with added values. These added values can take the form of other products or services. By association, their values can adhere to the product and reinforce its perceived worth. Their effect is to renovate the product, bumping up its potential ability to contribute to customer operating performance and financial performance.

A minimal system of added values contains six components. One will be the product that is being systemized. Incorporated with it will be traditional product-related services such as delivery, warranteed maintenance, repair, and replacement. Additionally, a system will include customer training and financing, perhaps with a lease or buy option. Together, these four components constitute a commodity system. Any competitive supplier under margin pressure can reproduce it. By themselves, the system's components are insufficient to ensure the differentiation that can be transformed into significantly improved customer profits.

Two more components are required if the commodity system is to be *branded*—that is, if it is to be given the capability to command a premium price based on premium value. For one thing, the system must contain a database of the customer problems and opportunities that will be solved as the means of improving profits. For another—and this is the most important of all—the system must be managed by a consultative sales representative who can improve customer profits with the system. The expertise and experience of the system manager, together with the accuracy and adequacy of the system's database, are the only components that permit differentiation. In the final analysis, they are the catalytic agents of every system.

In outline form, a typical branded system will look like this:

1. Consultative system manager
2. Customer database
3. The product
4. Product-related services
5. Customer training
6. Customer financing

Components 3 through 6 make a commodity system. Components 1 and 2 brand the system. They make it recompetitive. They give its commodity components the ability to maximize the improvement of customer profits. That is why they are placed first and second in the rank order of the system components.

Systemizing a product requires a dual renunciation. The product must be renounced in favor of a system. Then the system's performance value must be renounced in favor of the financial impact it makes on customer profits. The system's financial impact becomes the true "product," the end result of the system and its sole marketable output. The physical product, buffered by its system, has now been displaced by a financial product.

Systems sellers are marketers of financial values. They sell dollars of incremental profits to their customers. Their businesses, whatever their nature, undergo transformation to financial service businesses. They become manufacturers of customer profits. Their proposals are financial instruments. The values they propose to add to customer businesses are expressed in dollar terms: measurable, quantifiable over time, and more tangible to customers than even the physical products they have displaced. Nothing is more tangible than financial values because nothing else can be taken to the bank.

As a result, the decision to market the profitmaking capabilities of systems causes a business to be redefined. It must, in effect, go out of the manufacture of goods or services and enter the machining, the milling, the mining of customer profits. Henceforth, the business will be known by the customer profits it makes.

Systemizing a product is therefore a strategy to accomplish two objectives. First, the product is given renewed value by coupling it with additional products and services. Second, price is detached from the product. A stronger and price-less product results. The system will be a far more potent offering to its customers. Installed in their businesses, its multiple capabilities will make a considerably enhanced impact on the reduction of customer costs or the increase in customer productivity and sales. These will be the new performance values we will be supplying. Our price will be derived from them. It is imperative, then, that we resist the temptation to sell the system and concentrate instead on its financial values.

If we were to sell the system instead of its financial value to the customer, we would merely replicate our experience with the product. Its performance values would immediately be compared to competitive systems. So would its price. As the values matured, price would be pressured and margins shrunk. The net result would be an increase in the cost of our offering without commensurate increase in its contribution to profit. We would have escalated our asset base but not our return on its investment. We would have another and larger commodity on our hands.

2. Sell the Improved Financial Impact

Promoting and pricing systems is a zero-gain strategy. Systems, like products, represent only costs. They are a cost to their suppliers. They are a cost to their customers.

When a supplier tries to sell the cost of his system, he comes into head-to-head confrontation with customer cost containment. To be sure, his offering is more substantive than a naked product standing alone. It is able to solve more comprehensive customer problems. But it is still a cost seeking justification rather than a premium value meriting a premium price.

For a supplier who wants to be competitive in maturity, the sole marketable value of a system is its financial impact on a customer business. By marketing the system's ability to improve customer profits, a supplier confronts customer profit improvement, as opposed to customer cost containment. Here, increased bottom-line earnings rather than decreased purchasing costs are the objective. Decisions are value-based more than cost-based. Return is highlighted over the investment required to achieve it. The fairness of a price is determined by the rate at which it will be returned.

Systems are sold by not selling systems. They are sold by selling their contribution to enhanced customer profits. Commodity suppliers who are competitive in maturity invest their time, money, and human resources to *enhance the customer* and not to enhance their own product or its system. When they go to market, customer enhancement is what they take with them. For it, there is always a premium market. Not only does it differentiate the supplier who offers it and can deliver, it also differentiates the customer who uses it to grow.

Like products, systems have specifications. Like products, system specifications are performance characteristics. But system performance is calibrated in terms of financial values instead of operating values. There are two basic values that are important to every customer who wants to grow and whose growth we can leverage onto our own. One is incremental net profits, the amount of new earnings that can be added to the customer's business. The other is the rate of return these profits represent when they are compared against the investment that must be put up to bring them in.

An ideal system will deliver a financial impact composed of a high amount of new incremental earnings at a high rate of return. The earnings themselves measure the system's benefit. The rate at which they will be returned measures the system's productivity. Together, they enable customers to evaluate just how "good" a system is. They tell how the system "works." They define its "product." They make it deserving of a premium price or reduce it to a commodity.

3. *Attach Price to Profits*

Once a mature product has been displaced by new customer profits, price must be detached from the product or its system and affixed to the value of the profits. In this way, an altered value-to-price relationship can be created. No longer will price be limited to the parity performance values of a commodity product. Now price can be related to the unique profit performance of a system. The incremental profits that a system generates can form the revised basis for incremental margins.

In a commodity business, every product bears a price. The price defines the product. Its supplier calls it a fair price. Customers call it "too much." It forms the starting point of their adversarial purchase decisionmaking. The end point will be lower.

The physical products of a restructured business bear no price. They are, in this sense, free. They are necessary components of an integrated, comprehensive system from which they cannot be extracted and separately valued. Nor can the system as a whole be valued as the sum of the prices of its parts. The system itself bears no price. It, too, can be regarded as free. If it were to be priced, it would fall victim to the same cost-control process that customers apply to products. The whole purpose of systemizing would be lost.

If we are to regain competitiveness after maturity, we must value our systems the same way our customers will value them. *How much* do they contribute to customer profits? *How soon? How sure?* The answers will determine our systems' return. Price as such will disappear. In its place, as the correlate of return, we will substitute for price the concept of *investment*. Our systems will bear an investment cost. If their return is at a premium rate, the investment we require to yield it can be a premium, too.

Profits, in common with physical products, are priced according to their performance. They can be said to perform at a premium, thereby deserving a premium price, when one or more of three standards are met:

1. A lot of profits are produced.
2. Profits are produced fast.
3. Promised profits can be planned for.

A premium amount of profits merits a premium price. A premium rate of profit delivery merits a premium price. A premium certitude that profits will be available as planned merits a premium price. Because extra value is received in all three instances, an extra price is worth paying. In the first case, it is worth more to get more. In the second case, it is worth more to get more sooner. This relationship is known as the time value of money. It is based on the fact that today's dollar is always worth more than tommorrow's. Finally, in the third case, it is worth more to be sure that investment decisions made in anticipation of new profits can be committed in advance of the actual profits themselves. This acknowledges the value added by planning. It also recognizes the value of timely decisions for seizing transient opportunities and for avoiding opportunity loss.

Competitive maturity is dependent on a value-to-price ratio that relates premium price to premium value. The value, which must come first, is the basis for price. Product cost is made irrelevant. So is product performance. And so is competitive pricing based on product cost or performance.

Price, representing profit for the seller, can now be responsive to profit for the customer. No longer does the seller win only when the customer loses. Now, with the product displaced as the carrier of value and price, both supplier and customer can win new profits at the same time.

4. Finance the System

There are three basic methods of system financing. *Cash flow financing* is designed to optimize customer cash while a system is being paid for. The purchase plan can be geared to a customer's business income cycle. For businesses affected by seasonal ups and downs, a deferred or skip-payment schedule can permit smaller payments or even no payments at all during dry periods.

Two other financing methods are a *monthly service fee,* charged until the system's price is paid in full, and *leasing,* which permits system benefits to be enjoyed on a perpetual rental basis.

While these approaches differ, they share three similarities. They permit a customer to obtain the added values of a system immediately, without waiting until they can be afforded. In each case, a series of relatively small expenditures is substituted for what could be an undigestible big lump. The customer also has the option to purchase at any time.

There are two additional advantages worth noting in the service fee method. Because payment is extended over time, it may enable a customer to hedge somewhat against inflation. Another reason to defer payment is the possibility that the marketer will upgrade a system's performance characteristics during the life of the service fee. If this occurs, customers can benefit from new technical developments at no additional cost.

Like service fee financing, leasing is often an attractive alternative to outright purchase. Whereas service fees are a form of installment buying, leasing is a form of rental that enables a system's benefits to be acquired without the cost of possession. In addition, a lease customer can conserve cash and borrowing power. Leasing can be the preferred financing option whenever the profit on freed capital can outweigh a system's cost or whenever ownership of a depreciating asset is not an advantage.

5

Database the Customer

Recompetitiveness is data-dependent. It is dependent on knowledge of our customers' businesses: how much we know about their problems that we can solve most profitably and how much we know about opportunities to maximize their sales.

In order to become maturely competitive, three databased strategies must be followed:

1. We must identify our growable customers in terms of two characteristics: (a) the dollar values of their problems that we can solve and (b) their sales opportunities that we can help them achieve, together with the corresponding dollar values of our solutions.

2. We must penetrate our growable customers at the management levels where their problems can be most profitably solved.

3. We must prove the dollar values of our solutions and make these dollar values the basis for our price.

Each of these strategies for competitive profitmaking is dependent on customer data. Without accurate knowledge of the dollar values of customer problems and opportunities, we cannot know the dollar values of our solutions and the value-to-price leverage they can afford us, nor can we know the entry points where customer problems will be most profitable for us to solve. We will be flying blind, winging it. Our leverage for growth pricing will be lost.

A growth-customer database is our central resource for high-margin selling. It provides us with the two crucial targets we need for customer profit improvement: (1) the locations and amounts of customer costs that we can help reduce and (2) the locations and amounts of new sales revenues for our customers that we can help achieve. Without this knowledge, the transcendant admonition to "know our customer's business" has no meaning.

If we want to sell at growth margins, we must be able to perceive all customers' businesses the way customers themselves perceive them. For customers, a business is a collection of costs. Some of these costs are direct. They are business function costs. Dollar by dollar, customers can watch them erode profits. Every dollar of cost they can eliminate means more profit that can be dropped to the bottom line. Other costs are less direct. They are business opportunity costs. They are the losses customers are incurring from unrealized sales opportunities that could bring additional profits to their bottom line. These two types of costs compose the databases of customer businesses.

In order to grow our customers, we will have to internalize them in the form of a database that will bring their businesses into our business. In this way, our respective businesses can be merged into problem-solving partnerships. The customer's improved profit and our improved profit will become each partnership's common bond.

The APACHE® Datasystem

APACHE® is the acronym for a growth database. It stands for Account Penetration At Customer High-level Entry."* The APACHE datasystem is organized on a growth customer basis. It

* APACHE® is the registered trademark of Mack Hanan.

includes the 20 percent or so of all customer companies that account for up to 80 percent of our profitable sales volume.

Within each customer business, APACHE profiles two sets of data. One contains information on each business function where we have the capability to reduce or eliminate a customer's costs. The other contains information on each line of business where we have the capability to increase sales revenues.

Figure 5-1 shows a graphic representation of an APACHE database for an individual customer. The figure visualizes an APACHE database as if it were in manual form—which it may be to start—represented as two large portfolios. One contains customer cost problems organized by business function. The other contains customer sales opportunities organized by product line. Taken together, they represent "the customer" as far as our ability to grow that customer—and maneuver ourselves into a recompetitive position with him—are concerned.

APACHE is the source of answers to the fundamental question: How can we become competitive in maturity? We will become competitive by reducing the direct costs in our customer business function portfolios and by reducing the opportunity costs in our customer product line portfolios—that is, by increasing their product line sales. Either we will grow in these ways or we will not grow at all. Either the targets for our growth will be in our APACHE database or they will be unknown to us, unorganized by us, or unplanned by us.

An APACHE database proves our competitive dedication. If we are committed to restructuring, APACHE will be our shrine. It will attest to our determination to pull ourselves back from maturity. Without it, we can only pay lip service to recompetitiveness.

If we declare our dedication to growth, we must be prepared to pay it off with knowledge of *the sources that exist for our growth*. This is the starting point for recompetitiveness. There is only one place to which we can point. It is not to our products; they are mature. It is not to our systems; they are costs. It is not to our technology; it is at parity with our competitors. It must be to our markets. What it all boils down to is simply this: *Do we know how to grow our markets significantly enough to base a premium price on the value we add to their businesses?*

Figure 5-1. APACHE database.

If we are serious about growth, there will be an APACHE in our house. It will be the wellspring of our growth. We can compete for our customers' growth funds on the basis of our knowledge of how they can best be invested—better with us, because of the return we can provide, than in many other opportunities. If we lack this knowledge, all we can do is compete to become one of our customers' controlled costs on the basis of how low we can bid.

The APACHE–Profitmaking Partnership

APACHE is a stockpile of customer cost problems and revenue opportunities. It is, in effect, our profitmaking partner. The profit center managers and sales managers who compose our growth teams can use APACHE to answer questions like these:

"Tell me what you know about the power tool industry.

"What are the industry's growth trends and projections? How is it being affected by the current economic cycle? Let me see Black & Decker's position in the industry. How do they compare to the industry as a whole?

"Give me a closer look at Black & Decker's hand-held power tools division. What are its major lines of business? Which ones are the 20 percent that generate 80 percent or so of its profitable sales volume? Where are their major cost clusters? Give me the rank order of the power tool division's cost centers for hand-held tools arranged by business function. After that, give me the rank order of the division's sales opportunities for hand-held tools.

"What are the opportunity costs of being out of stock on retailers' shelves in big-winner items? What happens when these costs are added to the manufacturing costs of overproducing other items that sit on the shelves and don't move much at all—plus the administrative costs of controlling inventory, warehouse shipments, back orders, returns, and complaints? What is it most likely costing the hand-held tools product line to put up with these problems?

"Now let me work against the cost. What if we put together this forecasting and inventory control system? What will Black & Decker's investment have to be to obtain it? What annual rate of return will they get on their investment? What if we make this variation in the system: substitute this product or add this service? What improvement will that give their return? Is that the best return? The surest one? The fastest? If not, what is?

"Before I lock up my proposal, let me review all other proposals that have been presented on forecasting and inventory control systems for multiproduct manufacturing companies. What improved profits and rates of return did they propose? What systems did they sell? How does my proposal compare?"

Putting APACHE to Work

Dresser-Wayne is a manufacturer and marketer of retail management control systems. This is a mature business. One of its major lines is a cash management system for gasoline retail chains. It serves major oil company retail outlets and service stations, independent oil service stations, and convenience stores that also market gasoline. Except for convenience stores, these are mature markets. Dresser-Wayne's systems consist of gas dispenser pumps, electronic control consoles that operate and monitor the pumps, automatic cash registers, automatic service equipment, and data storage and handling capability.

To the individual gas station retailer, the benefits of Dresser-Wayne's systems are timely profit reports on sales, the flexibility to change pricing quickly to correspond to peak and off-peak driving hours, accurate cost control, inventory control, and reduced labor. The systems can also lower costs of station design by saving space and yet still increase the throughput of customer traffic.

The retailer's home office also benefits. It receives sales and inventory data faster and more accurately. The data can be used to reduce costs and improve sales revenue by optimizing the delivery schedules to each station. In addition, each supervisor at the head office can manage twelve stations instead of six, saving significant labor costs at a chain's supervisor levels.

The Dresser-Wayne sales force is equipped with an APACHE data system. Each market segment—the major oil companies, the independents, and the convenience stores—has its individual database. The general benefits that Dresser-Wayne can offer to all three segments are similar: improved profits through reduced costs and increased sales. But the specific benefits vary with the market segment. Accordingly, Dresser-Wayne's APACHE is organized to allow each sales representative to answer questions like these:

1. How can profits be improved at the station level? Is there an inventory problem with poor cash control? Is there a credit problem? Are receipts and distribution out of line? Or is there a problem of labor skills, quality of maintenance, or the efficiency of present station design and the resulting customer throughput?

2. Is this a product sale opportunity, a system selling opportunity, or an opportunity for the sale of a supersystem composed of several gas pumps, monitoring consoles, a cash management control system, data storage and handling modems, and a training program.?

3. Is this a lease or a buy opportunity?

4. Is there an opportunity to sell a plan to reconstruct individual gas stations to increase their traffic or is it more cost-effective to focus on improving station profit contribution from existing layouts?

5. How can profits be improved at the home office level? Is there a data control and reporting problem, or a problem with cash management or supervisory management?

6. What are the total costs to be reduced? What are the total sales revenues to be gained? What are the investment offsets required to achieve these results? What net profit is most likely to result to the customer and to Dresser-Wayne? What are the returns on investment?

The APACHE data system reports on the total number of outlets that can be affected in each chain, identifies each one as being among the top 10 percent, in the middle, or among "all others," and specifies the average number of gallons it moves each month, with other products and services. Data are also included on each station manager's purchase preferences, work force, and cost structure. Similar information is also available on home office managers.

Figures 5-2, 5-3, and 5-4 show what a Dresser-Wayne sales representative can see on the computer screen when he or she calls up the APACHE data. In Figure 5-2, he has called up the Midwest region of the ABC chain of convenience stores. When he asks for monthly profit contribution from each business function, he sees that inventory control is making a severe negative contribution. He wants to look at it in depth. Figure 5-3 shows what he sees next when he analyzes each of the component costs involved in inventory control. "Out of stock" costs jump out at him. In Figure 5-4, he has asked for a closeup look at the problem of stockout. This will give him the cost of being out of stock on an hourly, daily, weekly, and monthly basis. Now he knows the dollar value of the problem he can correct.

In the past, Dresser-Wayne used to sell products: gas pumps. Then its strategy was to sell groups of products and services in systems: control consoles, inventory gauges, automatic cash registers, and data modems, coupled with customer training and lease programs. In order to become competitive in maturity, Dresser-Wayne has had to transcend products, services, and systems to sell improved customer profitability. It has restructured from a "hardware" company that did business by moving iron to a "software" company that helps customers grow.

"The Customer in a Box"

For any business there are only two types of knowledge that can be used as a sales resource. One is an APACHE database that brings key customer knowledge into our business so that we can sell the same way our customers buy: from information about where their businesses need help. The other type is knowledge of our own product, based on benefits, features, and their costs. This knowledge is our own business. It does nothing to bring our

Figure 5-2. Problem/opportunity analysis by business function.

```
MARKET SEGMENT:  CONVENIENCE STORES
CUSTOMER:        ABC CHAIN, INC.
STATE/REGION:    MIDWEST




                           $ PROFIT CONTRIBUTION/MONTH
BUSINESS FUNCTION                  [PER STATION]

CREDIT CONTROL            $        269

INVENTORY CONTROL                [2,700]

CASH CONTROL                       240
```

Figure 5-3. Analysis of a single function.

```
BUSINESS FUNCTION:  INVENTORY CONTROL



                           $ PROFIT CONTRIBUTION/MONTH
SUBFUNCTIONS                       [PER STATION]

LEAKAGE                   $         40

VAPOR                               20

THEFT                              116


OUT OF STOCK                     [2,700]


EXCESS INVENTORY                   247
```

Figure 5-4. Analysis of a single subfunction.

```
BUSINESS FUNCTION:  INVENTORY CONTROL
     SUBFUNCTION:           STOCKING


                                                PER STATION


AVERAGE TIME OUT OF STOCK/HOURS                  ___06___

AVERAGE NUMBER GALLONS PUMPED/HOUR               ___75___

AVERAGE CENTS MARGIN/GALLON                      ___06___

AVERAGE NUMBER TIMES OUT OF STOCK/MONTH          ___10___


AVERAGE DOLLAR PROFIT CONTRIBUTION/MONTH         [2,700]
```

customer's businesses into our own. It does nothing to help us penetrate the top tiers of customer decisionmakers. With it, we can penetrate only as far as the purchasing level. At that point, we rapidly run out of consumers for knowledge of our business.

Because APACHE data is customer data, the top levels of customer decisionmakers speak its language. If our sales representatives use the same language, they will be able to claim an audience of top-tier customer decisionmakers. At these elevated entry points, the common denominator is not product knowledge but knowledge of how customers can improve their profits.

An APACHE data system is loaded with narrative facts. Its critical elements, however, are numbers: the dollar values of direct or opportunity costs in key customer business functions. Matching them, APACHE contains the dollar values of reductions in these costs or improvements in profitable revenues that can be provided by our solutions.

Customer problems and opportunities exist in numbers or they do not exist at all. If a cost or a chance to increase revenues cannot be quantified, if a number cannot be put on it, it will not exist in a business sense. For this reason, an APACHE database is a database of financial information where dollars are the predominant facts.

The quantification of a cost or opportunity attests to its significance. It tells how important it is. This assigns it a priority rank order for solution. If it is a cost, its dollar value tells how much it is subtracting from revenues. If it is a sales opportunity, it tells how much revenue is being lost. When numbers are large, they have salience. They communicate a degree of urgency. Even if the sum total of a large cost cannot be eliminated and only a small portion can be reduced, a small portion of a large cost can be significant. If the burden it imposes on profits can be relieved, immediate benefits can be conferred on the bottom line. The original cost, now lessened, can then be reduced a second time and more.

Quantification gives us our point of departure for growing our customers. The current cost customers are incurring right now is the "before" of our before-and-after growth strategy. The "after" measures what we have accomplished to make customers more profitable. It gives customers the chance to evaluate our contribution. They assess what they began with against what our growth partnership has done for them. It also assures us that we are playing our game. Both we and our customer can gain renewed confidence that our partnership is working, that we are growing each other, and that further growth can be expected.

APACHE tells us the two attributes of a cost or an opportunity we need to know in order to convert our knowledge into a growth event: *where* the cost or opportunity is, and *how much* money is involved. It remains for us to select the targets we can best attack from among its options. APACHE is a universe of growth targets. As little as 20 percent of them will reward our customers, and us, with 80 percent or more of growth. Our skill in selecting them will be the surest clue to our competitive capability.

The key to the selection process is for us to know "the numbers"—by how much can we affect our customers' costs and revenue opportunities? For this purpose, we will need to collect norms of our impact on customer growth. High norms reveal where we possess specialist skills in growing customers. These areas of our business are our true strengths, our real asset base for growth, and our most prized possession. If they do not compose 80 percent or more of our business, we are not managing our resources for the maximization of our growth.

The APACHE numbers and the qualitative facts behind them make it possible to take a competitive sales approach: to grow ourselves and grow our customers. Growing customer profit is not just a way to grow our own profit. It is the only way. This is win-win business management. Both we and our customers win new profits. Our customers win premium returns. In turn, we win premium prices based on their premium returns.

For this reason, APACHE must be the focal point of our recompetitive growth strategy.

V
CONSULT

6

Sell the Growth

Technology is never the source of restructuring into competitive maturity. Competitiveness is found in markets. Unless our customers grow, we ourselves will be unable to grow. We will have no one to grow us. Because recompetitiveness is dependent on customer growth, we dare not leave it to chance. We must help our key customers certify their growth and, along with it, our own.

In order to grow customer profits, we must create a key-account growth strategy. We must position our key account sales representatives as business growers for major customers. The "product" they sell must be a financial product: improved customer profit. Improved customer profit is the only product we can sell that will help our customers grow and, at the same time, grow us.

Product-driven managers believe that they can grow a business by offering "quality products." If their competitors had significantly inferior quality, they could get away with it. But where product quality is at parity, it cancels out. Service-driven managers believe that they can grow a business by offering "quality service." If their competitors had significantly inferior quality, they could get away with it. But where service quality is at parity, it cancels out. Process-driven managers believe that they can grow a business by offering "quality technology." If their competitors had significantly inferior technology, they could get away with it. But where technology is at parity, where innovation can be quickly replicated, it cancels out. Unless it is proprietary, science itself cannot, and does not, grow businesses. Nor can any other corporate function.

Product Value Derivation

In order for products to possess competitive value, they must add to customer profits. When applied to customers' business functions, products must be able to reduce their operating costs. They must reduce them significantly enough to make a difference. And they must reduce them dependably enough that the savings can be relied on. Similarly, products must be able to help customers increase their profits from sales of their own products. They must increase them significantly enough to make a difference, either by permitting the customer to sell greater volume at existing margins or to sell existing volume at greater margins.

Products must be developed, engineered, and manufactured with these objectives in mind. Customer cost reduction and customer sales increase must become the product specifications we design for. Our products "work" when, and only when, they meet a customer's profit-improvement specifications.

Does our product reduce a cost in a customer's business function? Does it reduce it significantly? Does it reduce it dependably? Can the reduced cost be quantified in dollars? If the answers are yes, the product "works" as a cost reducer. It can be represented as offering growth value to customers.

Does our product increase a customer's profitable sales? Does it increase them significantly? Does it increase them dependably? Can the increased profit be quantified in dollars? If the answers are yes, then the product "works" as a sales developer. It can be represented as offering growth value to customers.

Sometimes a product can offer a double growth value. It can reduce customers' costs and, at the same time, it can help increase profitable sales. If we can make a single product perform these multipurpose functions, it can free up customers' inventories. We can save them space. If we can counsel them on stocking the freed space with another profitable product, we can help them further increase their earnings from sales. We may be able to increase customers' productivity enough to free up one or more work hours a day per employee. If we can help customers convert this freed time to increased output and if we can help them market the output, they can obtain new earnings from sales.

To become competitive, we must redirect our traditional product thinking into two categories: Products are now "cost reducers" or "sales increasers." Some products may do both.

When we have classified our product lines according to their growth values, we will have a clear vision of our competitive positioning. Do we have products that grow our customers? Do they grow them enough, according to customer standards? Do they grow them more than competitive products? Are we principally *cost reducers for mature customers* or are we also *sales increasers for growth businesses*?

Customer Sales Growth

Cost reduction is essential to customer growth. But no customer can achieve growth by cost reduction alone. Sooner or later, generally sooner, he must grow more profitable sales volume.

Sales are the drive force of growth. If our product line is deficient in "sales increasers," it will leave us poorly positioned to accelerate competitive growth. Unless we can participate in the sales growth of our customers, we will never be able to play a vital role as growers of their businesses. We will be cut off from our customers' markets, the sources of their own growth. We will be deprived of knowing where their future growth is going to come from, how sizable it is most likely to be, what products they are required to offer in order to play a major role in their markets' growth, and what products we ourselves should be planning in order to maximize customer growth in the future.

If we have the ability to improve customers' productivity by reducing the number of employee hours required by one of their processes, we cannot rest with reducing their costs. We must help them find profitable use for the hours of work time we have released. We must become developers of new business for our customers if we are going to help them grow.

If we have the ability to improve customers' use of capital by reducing their inventories, we cannot rest with reducing their costs. We must help them find profitable use for the capital we have rescued. We must become developers of new business for our customers if we are going to help them grow.

Whenever we have the ability to reduce customers' costs, we must help find profitable investments for the dollars we have released so that they can put the money to work to make more money—more money than the free-up costs alone amount to. The best investment we can recommend ought to be with us, plowing back the customers' new profits into additional business. In this way, we can repeat the profit improvement process. Each time we complete a cycle of investment, return, reinvestment of the return, and additional return, we are providing capital to customers. This capital, generated from internal customer operations, will be the lowest-cost source of funds they can obtain. At each reinvestment stage, they will be using the funds that have been returned from their previous investment. Each investment in new profits pays for the next one.

Endlessly repeated, this is the *partnership cycle.* We prime the pump by making the first infusion of new profits into our customers' business. They reward us with a premium investment—new capital for us. Then we ask them to reinvest with us. With each transaction, we both grow.

Partners grow each other by stimulating each other's sales. What is true for our customers is no less true for us: competitive growth comes from profitable sales. We should seize every opportunity to improve customer sales. We should try to convert every reduction we make in a customer cost into a revenue opportunity supported by the time, the labor, and the dollars that we save. If we satisfy ourselves simply with cost savings, we leave the door open to our competitors. We invite them to become the beneficiaries of the high-margin profits that growth partnering allows. We will be downsized to the low margins of vendors. We will have given away our growthright.

Basing Price on Profit Values

When we sell improved profits to our customers, we help them reduce some of their main costs of operations or gain new sales revenues. Either way, the buyers of these benefits will now be higher-level decisionmakers who manage customer business functions. They are always in the market for improved profit contributions from the functions they manage. Their problems are defined in terms of contribution margins, net profits after taxes, and return on investment. Our product's price and performance values must become subordinated to the financial values that they can add to these components of the customer's bottom line.

The cost-benefit ratio of our product applications will be judged by customers on the basis of its impact on their profits. In other words, we will be evaluated as a supplier on the three how's of profit improvement:

1. *How much* do we help our customers grow?
2. *How soon* do we provide them with new growth profits?
3. *How sure* can they be that we will be a dependable growth source for them?

These three criteria of *How much, how soon,* and *how sure* are the operating standards of competitive maturity. We must be able to win on at least two of the three. If we offer large profit improvement to a customer, we must be prepared to make its delivery very sure. We need not deliver soon. If we offer less, we must deliver new profits both soon and surely.

The ability to sell high profit rewards at high customer levels is the prime growth skill. Only high value sales can yield the high margins that are essential for high profits. Two prior requirements must be met. First, an APACHE data system on the business problems and opportunities in key customer accounts must be in place. Then the key-account sales force must be trained in the three basic Consultative Selling® strategies of consultant positioning, profit improvement proposing, and decisionmaker partnering.*

Consultative Selling

Consultative Selling endows a mature company with a new growth tool. Instead of selling price-performance to purchasing managers, consultative sellers make profit improvement available at high margins to high-level customer decisionmakers. Instead of basing price on cost or on competitive prices, consultative sellers can base price on the value of the customer profits they improve— true value-based pricing. Instead of working principally from knowledge of their own business, consultative sellers work from knowledge of their customers' businesses. Instead of vending to purchasing managers, consultative sellers consult to top and middle management, the people who control the business functions whose profit contribution is to be improved.

How Consultative Sellers Grow Customers

"I'm Paula Brown, your profit improvement consultant," a consultative sale representative says, to begin her positioning with the top tier of a key-account customer. "My mission is to start today to work with you and your people on a close, continuing basis. I want to help improve your division's contribution to corporate profits by a million dollars over the balance of this calendar year.

"Profit improvement for your division is your mission, too. Both of us now have in common your most important business objective: adding new profits to your bottom line.

"I'd like to initiate our work together by proposing to you the first of what will be an ongoing series of Profit Improvement

*Consultative Selling® is the registered trademark of Mack Hanan.

Proposals.® I will be putting them together with the help of you and your people. My first proposal, like others to follow, is designed to reduce some of your costs.*

"My proposal is derived from homework on your industry, your company, and your division. Our homework has been organized into a database on your business. The database helps us pinpoint your major problems and opportunities, quantify their contribution to your costs, and then identify the single best solution. Our proposals come out of our database. They allow us to predict the dollar amount of new profits you can expect when we solve one of your problems. The proposals also itemize the exact strategies we will use to bring about the solution in your business.

"Each strategy mix will be custom tailored to solve a specific problem. Before you decide to accept it, I will be able to prove to you and your people how it will improve your profits and what the return on your investment will be. We will do this on paper in the form of a cost-benefit analysis so we can study it, understand just where the profits we will add are going to come from, and use it as a spec sheet.

"Before we sell you anything, we must both agree that the cost-benefit analysis is correct and that the system we have put together to solve your problem represents the optimal solution for you at this time. Once we install a system, I and my support team will work with your operating people to monitor its progress in improving your profits. We will improve it at once if we need to. Later on, we may want to upgrade it to provide even greater profit improvement.

"How long will we work together in this way? For as long as you want us to help improve your profits."

Consultative Selling Disciplines

Vendors use traditional commodity selling skills to move products on price, usually in high volume at low margins. Con-

---

*Profit Improvement Proposal® is the registered trademark of Mack Hanan.

sultative business growers use an entirely different set of skills that put them in a position that enables them to penetrate top-tier decision points and create problem-solving partnerships with customer decisionmakers.

They identify cost problems and sales revenue opportunities in customer businesses; they quantify their negative contributions to profit. They prescribe a solution; they quantify its positive contribution to profit. They sell the difference. In this way, they are able to achieve the objective of Consultative Selling: They can base their price on the value of the customer's improved profit.

How can vendor sales representatives become positioned as consultative business growers? There is only one way. To be positioned consultatively demands that a sales representative sell from customer business knowledge. Customer data is the consultant's calling card: it provides the ticket to partnership with high-level decisionmakers, and the basis for profit improvement proposing.

Consultative Selling is impossible without consultant positioning. This confers the ability to partner on a win-win basis throughout a customer organization. The crunch discipline, however, is the skill of defining a customer problem and calculating its solution, both in financial terms. This capability separates the true customer business growers who can actually improve customer profit from hybrid "consultative vendors" who verbalize profits in narrative form but who never present results that pay off in dollars.

The cost-benefit analysis format shown in Figure 6-1 is the consultative seller's proof that a customer's profit can be improved. The net profit and its rate of return that are being proposed answer the question, "Is this the best deal?" The cost-benefit analysis acts as a test for the solution, generating cost and revenue units on paper in advance of its performance in a customer's actual operations. If a proposed solution meets profit and return on investment objectives in the cost-benefit analysis, it "works." Its growth contribution has been proved. Now all that remains to be done is to make it work operationally in the customer's business.

Figure 6-1. Cost-benefit analysis.

Incremental Investment

1. Cost of proposed equipment $ _____
2. *Plus:* Installation costs   _____
3. *Plus:* Investment in other assets required   _____
4. *Minus:* Avoidable costs (repairs and re-
   modeling)   _____
5. *Minus:* Net cash proceeds after tax ad-
   justment for sale of properties re-
   tired as a result of investment   _____
6. *Minus:* Investment credit (if applicable)   _____
7. Total investment (sum of 1-6)   =======

Cost Benefit (Annual Basis)	A. Present or Com- petitive	B. Our Proposal	C. ± Dif- ference
8. Sales revenue (may be zero)	$____	$____	$____
9. *Minus:* Variable costs:			
10. Labor (including fringe benefits)	____	____	____
11. Materials	____	____	____
12. Maintenance	____	____	____
13. Other variable costs	____	____	____
14. Total variable costs (sum of 10-13)	____	____	____
15. Contribution margin (sum of 8-14)	____	____	____
16. *Minus:* Fixed costs:			
17. Rent or depreciation on equipment	____	____	____
18. Other fixed costs	____	____	____
19. Total fixed costs (17 + 18)	____	____	____
20. Net income before taxes (15 − 19) *	=====	=====	=====

Accounting Rate of Return on Proposed Investment

21. Total investment cost (line 7) $ _____
22. Average net income before taxes
    (line 20) *   _____
23. Before-tax rate of return
    (line 22 ÷ line 21) †   _____%

---

* If tax rate is known, calculate on after-tax basis.
† Average annual net income over life of the investment.

Mutuality of the Growth Objectives

Consultative Selling succeeds as a growth strategy where vending fails because vending is an adversary approach. It is win-lose. Price is the decisive element. If you pay my price, I win and you lose; if you pay less than my price, you win. Consultative Selling is win-win. Customer profit is improved while we earn a premium price that is commensurate with the customer's premium value.

Growth requires mutual objectives. We cannot grow for long by growing at customer expense. The more successful we are, the more certainly we will drive our customers out of business. Exploitation exploits the exploiter. For this reason, there is no "push" theory of growth. There is only "pull" theory, and it says the way to grow is to help our customers grow. They will pull us along with them into competitive growth.

How Customers Evaluate Growth

How will customers evaluate the significance of the new profits we sell them? The answer to this question is all-important. When we determine what our profit offering is worth, we determine our price.

Customers determine profit significance in two ways. One criterion is based on the return it represents. The second is based on the investment required to achieve it.

Return can be assessed according to four standards:

1. Its rate, compared with a customer's minimum hurdle rate or with the rate of return from competitive growth opportunities for the same investment.
2. Its volume, compared with a customer's profit gap or cash requirements.
3. Its timeliness, compared with a customer's cash flow needs.

4. Its certainty, compared with the 100 percent certainty of savings bank deposits or government money instruments.

Investment can be assessed according to three standards:

1. Its volume, compared with a customer's capital availability or with the cost of acquiring a similar infusion of capital through bank loans or equity indebtedness.
2. Its time value, compared with what the same investment will be worth when discounted over the time it will be unavailable.
3. Its payback, compared to how much money may have to be borrowed or taken from other investments before it is returned.

These are the customer hurdles to our positioning as a grower. If we can clear them, we can claim consideration as a growth partner. In doing so, we can regain our competitiveness.

7

Price the Profits

Before recompetitiveness, price is a mature product's sole differentiation. It occupies this dubious distinction by default. All other distinctions have been canceled out. Competitive performance benefits have become equalized. Equal values defy comparison. They permit only one inequality—the price at which they can be obtained.

With maturity, price comparison replaces performance comparison. The "best price" becomes the lowest price at which parity performance values are sold. They need not be better than competition. They simply must not be worse.

Shopping in a mature market is price shopping. Price is progressively forced down toward cost, which it soon comes perilously close to approximating. Vendors no longer represent performance values. They are known primarily for their cost. As a result, they find themselves incorporated into their customers' cost control systems. Even though they are an external cost, they will be controlled as if they were internal. This means they must pass the test of justification.

A cost that cannot be justified cannot be approved. Justification is achievable in two ways. A cost to be incurred must avoid or displace other costs. Or it must piggyback added values. In the absence of performance differentiation, values can be added to mature products only by packaging free services along with them. This provides the essential paradox of mature marketing. Services that are price-less in the benefits they confer bear no price. Products, however, are priced at no competitive advantage because they offer none. *Services are given away because the products to which they add value frequently cannot be.*

This is the essence of a commodity business. Its performance values serve only to maintain minimal price. Its service values may confer preferential purchase. But they rarely have the power to add to price to a degree that is in keeping with their worth or even with their cost. Mature prices resist all attempts to elevate them in either of these two ways. They can be maintained for a while. But there is no way they can be raised.

Once a business has become mature, price based on product performance values negates growth. It surrenders margin control, which should be the province of suppliers, to customer cost control. Price ceases to reflect the impact its product can make on a customer business. Instead, price represents the burden of our own investments and inefficiencies. It sums up what we have sunk into our asset base and our incapability to operate it at optimal cost-effectiveness.

Value-Basing Price

In order to be competitive in maturity, price must be divorced from our costs. It must be divorced from our operational inefficiencies. It must be divorced from parity performance values. And it must be removed from our customers' cost control systems. Where, then, shall we attach price?

If price is to return a growth margin, we must attach it to a growth value. This cannot be in our own product. It must be in the customers' business. The value of doing business with us must be translated into the value we add to the businesses of customers—the value of their growth to which we contribute.

Mature pricing says we add costs. What we add must therefore be as small as possible. Growth pricing, in contrast, says we add profits. We reduce customer costs in excess of our price. Or we increase customer sales revenues to a similar extent. These values we add should be as large as possible. If we attach our price to them, price can reflect their premium nature. At the same time, we will enter our customers' profit system and no longer be perceived as a cost to be controlled.

The detachment of price from our product, and thereby from its performance values, is the most crucial single step to growth.

Growth price can be referred to as value-based price as long as we remember the value we are using as our base: not product value but customer value; not the value of what we put into our product but the value we help our customers get out of it.

Pricing under a growth regime permits premium prices as long as we can deliver premium value. Margin control returns to our hands, dependent only on the extent to which we are able to improve customer profits. If we can improve them greatly, we can greatly improve our price on a cause-and-effect basis: Our improvement of customer profit is the cause; our premium price will be the effect.

Once our competitors and our customers no longer control our price, we are freed from dependence on "fair market value." Our customers can use price to reward us for growing their profits. Price will no longer be the penalty we pay for offering parity performance values. It will no longer represent the discount we involuntarily give to our customers for our lack of knowledge of how, or by how much, we can improve their profits. Price will be our reward. It will be the investment we receive for the return we deliver.

Growth pricing removes our price from a product or process base. It puts it on a financial basis. Our price can move from a cost-plus relationship to a relationship to customer profit. Price can stand for a new money value. It can say to our customers that this is the worth of the new money we are making available to them.

Customer decisionmakers above the purchasing level are used to "buying money." They are familiar with the cost of capital. They know the prime rates for borrowed funds. They understand the tradeoff between a return and the investment required to

Figure 7-1. Profit tradeoffs in Brand Country.

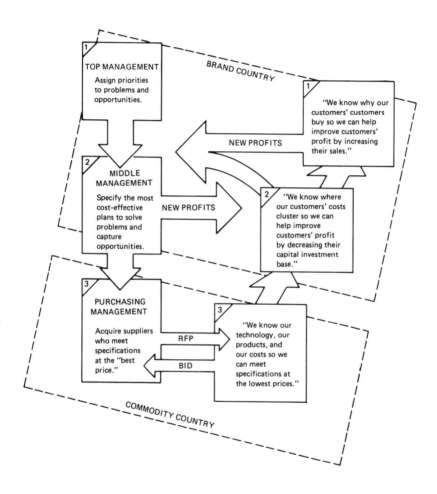

achieve it. They are almost universally willing to buy money from us at a significantly higher price than they would ever pay for our products.

This is the way business is done in Brand Country, as Figure 7-1 shows. When a branded business transaction takes place, it is new dollars of profit, not products, that are being exchanged.

The customer, whose management hierarchy is shown on the left in the figure, receives new profits from the supplier. These are the results of the financial impact the supplier makes on the customer's business by what is sold. In turn, the supplier receives new profits from the customer. These are the results of the premium margins the customer pays in return for having profits improved.

For the customer, receiving premium profits merits paying a premium price. For the supplier, delivering premium profits merits receiving a premium price. The supplier becomes branded as the customer's profit-improver. This, more than any product or service distinctions that suppliers may try to create, differentiates them from competitors who, in Commodity Country below, are still transacting products.

In Brand Country business, pricing is really investment pricing. Price is not presented, nor is it perceived, as a cost. It is an investment: an expenditure on which there will be a return that will exceed it. In competitive maturity, just as the physical tangible product must be displaced, so must the concept of price as a cost.

When they buy our money, customers can put it to work at once. They can invest it in growing their businesses, adding to their assets, or paying off their liabilities. When they buy our products, though, they must first convert our performance values to cash values. To do this, they must commit direct costs of their own. These subtract from the eventual cash value of doing business with us. They must also incur the time cost of waiting for the conversion of performance values to cash values to take place. These costs further subtract from their eventual reward. Finally, our customers may be inefficient in making conversions of our product values into cash. They may lost value along the way, subtracting even more from their ultimate profits. It is easy to see why they will be willing to pay us more when we can reduce their direct cost commitments, condense the time before their new profit values flow to them, and prevent lost values by counseling with them on optimizing our product applications.

Reducing customer costs improves profits. Shortening the waiting time for profits also improves them. Increasing operating productivity within customer business functions increases profits yet again. These are the benefits our prices should charge for, because these are the values our customers will pay a premium to obtain.

Growth Pricing over the Life Cycle

A growth price is a premium price. Its high unit margin frees us from dependence on volume as the multiplier of profits. It also sets us apart as the perceived value leader.

The ability to price at a premium is conferred by our markets. We can, and must, plan for it. They, however, make the final disposition. Their decision will be based on two considerations:

1. Do we offer lower life cycle cost as the tradeoff against higher initial cost?
2. Do we offer higher life cycle sales revenues as the tradeoff against higher initial cost?

These are the two crucial evaluations we must survive. They are our gateways to competitive maturity. Our competitiveness depends on how well we understand the customer's tradeoff of initial cost against life cycle cost.

For our customers, combining low life cycle cost with premium initial price enables them to benefit at once from our product. In the present value of their eventual payback, they have a rationale for immediate purchase. From our perspective, the combination provides us with early cash flow and eased market penetration.

Figure 7-2 represents the combination of high initial acquisition cost with low operating and maintenance costs that makes premium profits for our customers over their life cycle of use. Since lowered life cycle cost justifies a high acquisition cost, maximum customer uptime must always be a pricing objective. This is the intermediate objective that leads directly to the customer's ultimate goal of maximum contribution to profit. Maximum up-

Figure 7-2. Acquisition cost–life cycle cost: ideal relationship.

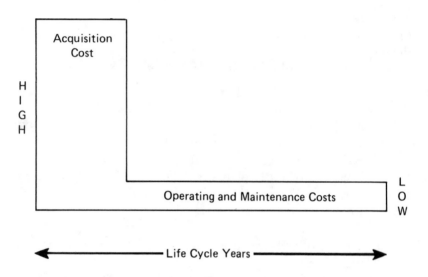

time is a positive-thinking way of expressing the intermediate objective; minimum downtime says the same thing but in a negative manner. No customer wants downtime, even a minimum. Every customer wants maximum uptime.

Customers buy uptime one way or another. They pay for it up front in the form of premium price. Or they pay for it as they go along, repair by repair and replacement by replacement. Paying for uptime up front is a direct cost. Paying for it on a pay-as-you-go basis represents an opportunity cost to customers. What they lose in sales, what they pay in idle labor, what loss of market share and reputation they suffer from unshipped customers, can far exceed the one-time direct cost of a premium price.

Reliability must, as a consequence, become every competitive company's middle name. Without reliability there is nothing to sell. Nor will there be any basis for sales strategy because there will be no way to trade off low life cycle cost against high purchase price.

Reliability as Our Middle Name

To be middle-named reliable, we must do more than build low operating and maintenance costs into our products through self-diagnosis and self-repair, modularity, and redundancy. We must also support our products with training programs for customer personnel, a repair and replacement policy that is market-driven and not driven by our legal or accounting departments, and a warranty program.

Reliability is also the principal means of supporting a premium purchase price by improving customer profits through increased sales revenues. If we choose this option, our reliability will have to be directed toward two objectives. First, our product must help increase the reliability of our customers' products so that they, too, can justify a higher purchase price with their own customers. Second, the added benefit we provide must be reliably delivered so that both our customers and our customers' customers can depend on receiving improved profits every time.

In these two ways, we can aid customers to bring in new sales revenues at higher margins.

The Individuality of Price

When price is based on cost or "fair market value"—a euphemism for the lowest competitive bid—a price list can be used to answer the question, "How much?" Standard products will bear standard prices. Brand pricing eliminates the price list. When branded offerings are sold, there is no price. The investment that is required to obtain them is individualized, never a generalization. It is specific to each customer because it is specific to the return on investment he will receive.

Value-based pricing, or customer-based pricing, individualizes each sale. It acknowledges that all customers are different. Their costs in the business functions that we can reduce are different. The amount by which we are able to reduce them will be different. The value they assign to what we do for them is different, too. In the same way, their sales revenue growth opportunities will be different. So will the increases in revenues that we can help them achieve and the value that they will assign to each increase.

No customer relationship can take place under competitive maturity without first studying each customer's business to determine this individuality. This is in marked contrast to mature business relationships where all customers are presumed to have the same needs: They all buy on price and so they all need the lowest price and the highest performance. The correlate of this assumption also pervades customer perspectives. Customers in mature markets assume all suppliers are pretty much the same except for price. In their attempts to be amiable, mature suppliers make this assumption self-confirming.

Competitive maturity challenges these assumptions. All customers are not alike. Some can have their profits improved more than others. Some are willing to pay more for it than others. All suppliers are not alike, either. Some can improve customer profits more than others. Some can do it faster or more reliably than others.

Individualizing customer relationships is a hallmark of competitive maturity. It makes sure that a database will be developed on each customer's growth potential and that customer-specific proposals will be created out of its information. It demands that each customer relationship on which competitive maturity depends will be a one-to-one type of partnership in which the growth of both partners can proceed in parallel.

8

Partner the Growables

There are two types of natural partners for recompetitive growth. One is customers we are already growing; we are improving their profits right now. In some cases, we may be aware of our contribution but our customers may not. More likely, it is our customers—not us—who will be aware that they are growing because of us. Their profits are being improved, but we are not benefiting. Our prices are vendor prices. Our sales are derived from competitive bids, not partnered proposals. We are growing them but they are not growing us.

The second type of natural partner for our growth is customers who are growable by us but whom we are not currently growing. We may not be aware of who they are, perhaps because we do not have criteria for selecting them. They do not know who we are, either. We have not promoted our growth capability to them. Neither of us is growing the other. As a result, both of us are incurring opportunity loss.

Identifying Partners

Market segmentation is the process of selecting our growth partners from all others—identifying our *growing customers* and our *growables* and concentrating our growth with them.

Growth partnering is market segmentation made easy. Does a customer have cost problems that we can help reduce? In other words, are we experts in the cost-effective operation of business functions on which the customer depends? If we are, then that customer is partner material. Does a customer have sales opportunities that we can help achieve? In other words, are we experts in the cost-effective development of sales to the markets on which the customer depends? If we are, then that customer is partner material.

When we partner, we segment our market according to who benefits from our expertise. When we vend, we sell to whoever buys our product. In partnering, we look for customers to enrich. In vending, we look to enrich ourselves. As a partner, we and the customer together compete against the customer's current standards of cost management and revenue production. As a vendor, we compete against other vendors.

In order to grow our business, we must segment it in two cuts.

In the first cut, we will segment our growing customers and our growable customers out of our total universe of customers. These segments will be our *growth partners*.

In the second cut, we will segment twice. First, we will select the costs we can reduce in the business functions of our growth partners. Second, we will select sales opportunities we can increase in the markets served by our growth partners. This will segment our *growth strategies*.

As a result, we will never again have to ask who our growth sources are: They will be built into our business. We will know their needs from the outset: They will need cost reduction or sales increases. Nor will we ever have to ask what our growth strategies should be: Either we will be reducing a customer cost or increasing customer sales. We will have no other options. There will be no other strategies we can employ for growth and no other customers with whom we can employ them.

Partnering Prerequisites

Customers who become our growth partners will be the primary sources of our growth profits. But before we can become operational with them as their partner, we must meet four prerequisites:

1. Mutual Objective

Growth partners must have the same objective. Each must grow the other. The customer partner's growth is transcendent. It must be the superior objective of the partnership because it is the source of the supplier partner's growth. If the customer grows, he will grow the supplier by demanding more growth. Otherwise neither will grow.

A partnership's foremost growth objective is always the customer partner's objective. This gives growth partnering its uniqueness as a business relationship. Two companies work for the objective of one. They dedicate themselves to growing the customer partner, who becomes the basis of the partnership's growth.

This is in marked distinction to traditional vendor relationships where, instead of acting as partners, vendors and their customers are combatants in a win-lose relationship, both trying to impose their objectives on the other. The customer seeks the lowest cost of goods. The supplier wants the highest margins. If either one is to grow, it must be at the expense of the other.

Partners win by enhancing each other. Mutual enhancement requires a mutual objective: *Grow the customer first.* When partnerships work, it is because the customer is being grown. When partnerships fail, the mutuality of their objective has fallen away and the partnership is atomizing into separate interests.

Customers who have never partnered find it difficult to believe that suppliers will actually commit to their customers' growth. Suppliers who have never partnered find it difficult to maintain their commitment, lapsing back into merchandising their products, wrapping them in purchase orders, and pricing them on their performance benefits. Moving product does not grow customers. It serves them, sells them, and stocks them, but it does not grow them because it costs them. Only the new profits of growth will enhance them.

2. Mutual Strategy

Growth partners must agree on strategy, on how the partnership will grow the customer. Both partners must know their roles. What resources will they contribute, who will manage them, how will they be evaluated and rewarded? Since every resource adds a cost that raises the breakeven point of the partnership, strategy must always be minimal.

Knowing how the customer's improved profit will be achieved enables the partners to set up a control system to monitor growth on a progressive basis. Attaining each growth milestone "on plan" announces that the partnership is working.

Strategy can be measured—or, for that matter, managed— only if it is explicit. It is not a strategy simply to say that we will reduce inventory cost. How will it be done? Will labor or materials costs be reduced? Insurance costs? Security costs? Energy costs? The costs of tied-up capital? Will materials handling be made more cost-effective, will space requirements be reduced, or will turnover be increased? By how much? Within what time frame?

3. Mutual Risk

Growth partners share the risk of partnership. The quintessential risk is failure to achieve mutual growth, the very reason for the partnership's existence. If lesser growth is realized, the opportunity represented by the partners' objective has been lost.

Mutuality of risk means that both partners can fail, but not necessarily equally. In fact, equality of risk will rarely be the case.

Customers will almost always perceive their risk to be greater. They will lose profit. They will lose market share. They will lose competitive position.

The suppliers' loss will be almost as severe. From the small and irreplaceable segment of partnerable customers, one of them will be lost, perhaps forever.

In order to equalize risk, supplier partners must assume more than 50 percent of a partnership's responsibility. After all, it is they who instigate partnership; they must warrant its feasibility. This can be fortified by positive answers to four questions:

1. Is this customer superior partner material because the customer is being grown significantly by us right now or is growable?
2. Are this customer's business functions susceptible to significant cost reduction or are the customer's markets suceptible to significant revenue improvement?
3. Are these objectives achievable at a level that is significant to the customer?
4. Is a strategy available to us that is cost-effective yet capable of maximizing our achievement of these objectives?

There is also a fifth question, to minimize risk to the supplier: If the objectives are achievable for the customer, will our own growth objectives be achieved as a result? Otherwise the supplier will forsake business for philanthropy.

4. Mutual Reward

Growth partners who share risk must also share reward. As with risk, reward will rarely be equal. The customer partner will profit more than the supplier partner. But the supplier will profit more in the role of partner than vendor. The relationship will be win-win.

The mutuality of profit reward is paramount. Subsidiary rewards abound. Customers obtain a dedicated supplier. The supplier's growth team learns the functions of the customers' businesses, knows how they contribute to customer profit and how to improve the contribution. The supplier's team becomes a priceless customer resource. Not only does it grow new profits, but it also works on behalf of its customers without direct compensation.

For their part, suppliers obtain dedicated customers on whom profit is disproportionately dependent. They gain access to their customer partners' high-level decisionmakers and to the proprietary knowledge they possess of their businesses. This access is privileged, denied to competitors. The suppliers' margins are similarly protected at a high level. As long as they continue to grow their customer partners, they can protect their margins against vendor erosion.

Operating a Partnership

Partnerships are profit maximizers. That is how the partners grow each other and, in turn, grow themselves. The volume of profits that they generate is paramount. A partnership that is a heavy profitmaker is to be preferred to a light earner, and a consistently heavy profitmaker is the most preferred.

Earning profits in volume maximizes growth. Earning profits quickly and recurrently minimizes the time within which growth takes place, magnifying the time value of money. A third consideration is the certainty of growth.

Growth partners have similar needs. They both want maximum cash flow and they want it on a dependable, continuing basis. This is the motivation that brings them to partnership. But method differs from motivation. The method by which both partners prosper is for both of them to grow the customer partner. The customer is the sole provider of partnered growth.

The prime objective of growth partnerships is the maximized growth of the customer. This is not merely a supplier's sales strategy. This is partnership operating strategy. It permits no deviation. To lapse from it is to relapse into vending. All objectives for the partnership must therefore begin with growing the customer. The supplier's growth is derived growth, the result of customer growth and totally dependent on it. Without the one, there is none of the other.

Tests of Partnering Significance

Partnering is profitable, and affordable, only with customers who represent significant growth. These are the customers to whom we are contributing major profits right now. They are also the customers whom we have the potential ability to grow in the near-term future.

The Partner Selection Test

Each customer from the two groups mentioned above should meet the three segmentation criteria of the partner selection test.

1. *Significance of Profit Contribution.* A partnership must provide a minimal annual profit. The minimum profit equals or exceeds the partners' hurdle rates for return on investments in their own businesses. Minimal annual profit will depend on the answers to two questions:

- Does the customer have significant costs in major business functions that we can significantly reduce?
- Does the customer have significant sales opportunities in major markets that we can significantly increase?

2. *Continuity of Profit Contribution.* A partnership must provide profit accumulation that can be forecast over at least a three-year life cycle.

3. *Growth of Profit Contribution.* A partnership must provide an increasing annual rate of profit increase over its life cycle so that it remains a blue-chip investment option for both partners.

These three criteria will help determine if a customer qualifies as a prospective partner. In this respect, growth partnering forces us to evaluate our customer portfolio according to profit criteria, not volume or our participative share of a customer's business as an alternate vendor.

Growth partnering also stimulates four additional tests of significance about our products, our technology, our data, and our management:

The Product Test

1. Can our product significantly reduce a significant customer cost?
2. Can our product significantly increase significant customer sales?

The R&D Test

1. Can our technology commercialize products that significantly reduce significant customer costs?
2. Can our technology commercialize products that significantly increase significant customer sales?

The Database Test

1. Do we know the dollar values of the costs we can significantly reduce in the customer business functions we significantly affect—and do we know the dollar values of our solutions?
2. Do we know the dollar values of the sales opportunities we can significantly increase in the customer markets we significantly affect—and do we know the dollar values of our solutions?

The Management Test

1. Do we have the profit-center managers and sales managers who can apply our products, support systems, and database to significantly reduce significant customer costs?
2. Do we have the profit-center managers and sales managers who can apply our products, support systems, and

database to significantly increase significant customer sales?

The Limits of Maturity

Mature businesses find their natural trading partners in other mature businesses. Culture attracts culture. So does bigness. A volume producer needs a volume user; a volume user needs a volume producer. At first, it appears to be a salubrious relationship. But it is the kiss of death for growth. As the Japanese have said about mature companies doing business with each other, "The only business relationship they know is to quote prices and then ship parts."

Maturity predisposes mutual concern for cost control, not sales improvements. Cost-heavy producers control unit cost with volume. The more they manufacture, the less each unit costs. Their customers control cost by enforcing competitive bidding. The less they spend, the lower their costs will be. In these terms, a successful transaction is one that limits the damage to both sides. Fortunate suppliers come away with sufficient margin to fund the next manufacturing cycle. Fortunate customers come away with funds they have managed to hold onto that they can invest somewhere else.

Under these conditions, no one is growing anyone. Mature suppliers are fixated on justifying the transfer of their costs to customers in the form of price. Mature customers are equally fixated on resisting the transfer.

When mature-business managers think about growing their customers, it is usually too late. At that point, they can no longer sell to them at surviable margins. Customers are merging, shrinking, or divesting. A combination of high costs and low-priced competition is driving them out of business. If they are going to survive, their suppliers must help them by reducing price. It then becomes the suppliers' turn to merge, shrink, or divest. Mutual negative growth is the inevitable result.

Some suppliers see the handwriting on the wall. They realize that there is no way they can make a market in slow-growth or no-growth relationships. Customer cost reduction becomes their objective. Instead of lowering their prices, they justify them by calculating the customers' costs they can displace and proving them to be greater than their prices. They become experts in cost reductions. This helps their customers improve profits, enhancing their viability and ensuring survival for a while longer. But viability and survival are not growth. Unless customers can be helped to increase their profitable sales, little real growth can occur.

To do that, suppliers and customers must become experts in stimulating customer markets. As the customer grows, so grows the partnership. As the partnership grows, so grows recompetitiveness.

Appendix A

Recompetitiveness Doctrine

1. *Agreement on Objective of Becoming Recompetitive*

1.1. The principal objective of a business is to grow profit.

1.2. The principal objective for growing profit is to be self-financing in capital generation.

1.3. The principal means of growing profit is to command premium price.

1.4. Therefore, the principal task of management is to create and recreate businesses that can command premium price.

2. *Guidelines to Recompetitive Pricing*

2.1. The basis for premium price is market perception of premium value.

2.2. A recompetitive price is based on added value to the user, not added value to the product. This added user value can be computed as a positive return on the user's investment to acquire the added value.

2.3. A recompetitive value-to-price ratio must always favor user value. When price is compared against the return on investment that is represented by price, value must be in excess of price.

3. *Role of Marketing in Becoming Recompetitive*

3.1. Marketing is the principal brand-building function of a business. Marketing is the only function that can create the perception of added value to the user in the minds of a market.

3.2. The principal marketing capability for becoming recompetitive is knowledge of the user values that can be added to a market. There are two main user values: improvement through reduced costs and improvement through increased productivity and sales revenues.

3.3. The marketing of improved customer profit is a win-win function. The market wins by gaining access to premium value. The marketer wins by gaining command of premium price.

Appendix B

Branding to Retain Present Competitiveness

Branding is the strategy of user differentiation. By enriching our customers, we differentiate them. We give them new wealth that enhances them and makes them stand out from their competitors. We make them "best." Or we give them new power that enables them to control their personal or business life-styles, make them more productive and predictable, and allow them to reward those who depend on them. We brand them with the twin cachets of success: richness and distinction.

In the process, we brand ourselves as different, too. We are no longer one of several alternate vendors, each with a parity product whose only true variation is price. We are growers. As such, we can identify branded customers when we see them. Someone is growing them by improving their profit. We can tell when we are branded, too. We are being grown by our customers. They are paying us premium unit price.

There are, accordingly, two definitions of branding. The customer's definition says that branding is the profit difference between the customer's business and the competition. The supplier's definition says that branding is the ability to command premium price by conferring premium profit on customers. For both customers and their suppliers, branding is the same: *user differentiation.*

Branders deal in values, not products. To say the same thing in another way, branders' products are not physical, tangible hardware but physical, tangible profits for their customers. Branders sell money, new money that their customers would not have available to them without a brand partnership. Instead of asking, how can we sell this customer? branders ask, how can we grow this customer, how can we add value to this customer's business, how can we improve this customer's profits?

Customer-Specific Values

Unlike vendors, each of whose products bears an off-the-shelf price, branders' prices originate with each customer. This means that there is no price that can be placed on a brander's value until the value has been calculated for a customer's business. Each value is customer-specific. Branders, as a result, do not publish a price list. Nor do they sell products from a catalog.

On the shelf, a brander's products represent only costs. If these costs were simply to be transferred to customers in the form of price, the brander would become a commodity vendor. Instead, *branders create value.* Partly through the performance of their products, partly through the customer knowledge and applications expertise of their people, branders come into the businesses of their customers and create values that were not there before. When they have finished, their customers have greater worth.

There is no way to value branders except by performance. That is why proof of performance as a profit-improver is so vital to branding, especially proof of a track record and proof in the form of a cost-benefit analysis that shows how the track record can be applied to a specific customer's business. This accounts for the highly personal, individualistic relationship that each customer has with a brander.

Even though branders serve many customers in the same industry, they create different values for each of them. Customers who have never worked as partners with branders may ask, will you do the same thing for my competitors? If, by the same thing, the customers mean will branders improve competitor profits, the answer is yes. But the answer is no if they are asking whether all competitors will have their profits improved in the same amount within the same time at the same degree of certainty. If that were the case, branders would be commodity vendors.

Branders leave their customers no choice but to value them on the net worth they create. These values come from branders' systems when they become operational within a customer's business. The branders enter a customer's manufacturing function, for example, reduce the cost of a process, and create a new value. Or they enter a customer's marketing function, increase the sales revenues from a market, and create a new value. The new values that are created have been planned in advance. There are no surprises. Branders have based their price on them. The branders' customers have based their value-to-price relationship on them. They have already planned how to reinvest the new values. Some portion of the reinvested values may be with the brander so that another cycle of profit improvement can be initiated; in vendor terms, the customers will reorder.

In such an event, customers are no longer playing with their own money. They are using incremental funds that their branders have created for them—money that does not have to be drawn off from operating funds or reallocated from other priorities. This may be the greatest value that branders provide.

Putting a Value on the Value

No matter how much branders learn about the businesses of their customers, the customers will know one thing that branders must discover anew with every transaction. Branders know how much value they can add, but only the customer can put a value on the value; only customers can tell branders what their value will be worth. Branders are able to say, "I can improve your profits by $100,000." It is up to the customer to say, "That will be worth $250,000 to me in 18 months."

A customer will always set a value that is higher than a brander's face value. Branders deal in *applied value*. Customers take applied value and multiply it to its second derivative, *investment value,* which they calculate based on what they plan to do with the applied value. They may invest it in their own businesses. Or they may invest it outside. Either way, they will use it for growth. The net worth of that growth will be the customers' concept of true value.

In business, value is used to beget value. Money makes money. Circulation of capital depends on the turnover principle for the velocity by which value is generated. The more money that can be circulated, the greater the multiplier effect of turnover can be. Branders affect both components of the capital circulatory system. They bring more money into the system. They also help customers turn it over faster by providing premier opportunities for investment.

The customers' invested value—what it will amount to when it is calculated as "future value"—and not the branders' applied value, should be the basis of brand price.

Future value is the total value that will accrue over time as the result of a present investment. Time is therefore of the essence. The faster the brander can create values in customer businesses, the sooner customers can invest them to make more. For this reason, because money exists only in the context of time, there can be no consideration of dollar values without their time values.

Long time frames without payout devalue money just as short time frames enrich its value. Branders' definition of *what* they sell—money—is never complete without their definition of *when* it will be avaliable for use.

Vendors are constrained to deliver their product values on time. So are branders. For them, being on time involves more than having physical products on a customer's receiving dock. It means having new dollars in the customer's till. This is the function of the brander's application skill. Nothing happens to make a customer more profitable if only a shipping date is met. That simply transfers a cost from supplier to customer. Until a customer's business functions are affected—until a brander's appliers make their applications so that a cost is reduced or sales revenues are increased—value will remain to be seen.

Because branders' value is applications value, it is clear that branders are beholden to their applications experts. They hold the branders' brand posture, control their effectiveness as branders, and stand between brandedness and the yawning pit of becoming a vendor.

When customers buy brands, they are really buying a brander's applications experts, the teams of consultative account representatives plus their technical, financial, and data support staffs. No brander can be better than they are. No matter how heavily capitalized a brander may be, branding is a labor-intensive business. Capital cannot apply itself; only people can apply it. Capital cannot create partnerships with customer function managers; only people can partner. Capital—even in the form of product values—cannot brand; only people can brand the customer values on which branding depends.

The Futility of Branding Product Values

The cycle of investment and reinvestment of brand values is unique to branding. It is impossible to accomplish with product values alone. This is why vendors must make every sale all over again as if it were the first sale. They lack inherent continuity because they cannot quantify the customer values, if any, that their products contribute. They pay the price for seeking to differentiate their products instead of their customers.

To the same extent that branders are obsessed with their customers and making them into winners, vendors are obsessed with their competitors and making them into losers. Branders try to enhance the objects of their obsession; vendors try to diminish them. To do this, they enhance themselves, their products, and the processes by which they are made.

Secret or exclusive ingredients, magic formulas, and exotic formulations—"contented cows" from Borden's and the father-and-son assembly teams of Studebaker—are historically invoked by vendors to distinguish their parity products from all others. Continental Can's "Econoweld" is American Can's "Miraseam"; each welds tin-free steel cans seamlessly. Each adds similar value to the product. But what is the unique value added to the customer? Unless there is an answer to this question, each will have to be sold on product value. Since both products have been equally valued, price will be equal, too.

In the past half century, only two major products have been successfully branded on the basis of value that has been added to them. One was Xerox copiers; the other was Polaroid instant cameras. For approximately a generation, each commanded a brand price. But neither could prove a unique customer value to support a brand price when less expensive competition ended their honeymoons. They became commodities virtually overnight. Neither has ever recovered.

Because brand values are customer values, no one covets them more than customers themselves. In contrast, only vendors covet their product values. They explain them through infinite detail, exhibit them in closeup microphotographs and cutaway drawings, and exalt them in purple prose. When they finish, customers ask, "How much?" When they reply, customers say, "Too much." The only way that customers can create added value is to reduce the vendors' added cost, their price.

Three Forms of Enriched Value

The value that a brander can add to customers may take three forms. The most straightforward form is *improved profits*. They are always desirable, preferable by far to any other value by a

profitmaking business. They are advantageous for two other reasons as well. Profits are accurately measurable and immediately investable. They are the closest a customer can come to instant growth. This is equally true for the brander since the customer's profits—being measurable and investable—are immediately priceable.

A second form of customer value is *improved productivity*. It is specifically important to nonprofit and not-for-profit customers. Improved productivity provides incremental performance advantages. People and functions operate more cost-effectively. Either more output results from the same asset base or a smaller, reduced asset base yields the same output. Productivity is measurable, although not with the same exactitude as profits. But it is not always translatable into a value. Operating more cost-effectively is an acceptable objective if growth is to be achieved through cost reduction. Productivity brings costs down. Growth, however, depends on more than just elevated productivity. It depends on developing a demand base for the added capacity. Otherwise, productivity gains lead to unanswerable questions such as "How do we utilize the one-third of the staffer we have just freed up?"

A third value is *improved pride*. It is neither measurable nor investable. Nonetheless, it is demonstrable in such business attributes as heightened incentive, better morale, and even greater productivity. While feeling good and working good are not necessarily one and the same, feeling good may help reduce absenteeism, turnover, downtime, rejects, and callbacks. This, in turn, may have an improved effect on profits. Affecting pride alone is a brander's weakest position. But pride value is a worthwhile additive to profit value. In combination with productivity value, two unmeasurables do not add up to strength but their reinforcement effect on each other may accomplish what neither alone can do: brand a customer and merit a premium reward for the brander. To pledge allegiance to "total quality control," "excellence," and the old standbys of reliability and dependability may instill pride internally and even improve productivity. But the proof of their brand value is in the new dollars they generate, first for customers and then for their suppliers.

Taking a Branded Posture

Branders can add value to any business whose costs they can reduce or whose sales revenues they can increase by playing "our game"—applying their expertise and systems to customer operations where they are process-smart and to customers' customers where they are market-smart. In order to set themselves apart as *"the* people who do this," branders must take a unique posture in their markets.

While vendors are praising themselves and condemning their competitors, branders are partnering with customers. Vendors try to isolate themselves from their me-too lookalikes. Branders try to ally themselves with growth partners, the customers whose growth will determine their own. But branders, no more than vendors, cannot simply legislate partnerships nor can they grow someone else's business uninvited. They must first demonstrate their capabilities. What are the base abilities of branding? There are three: the ability *to apply growth* to a customer, the ability *to teach growth* to a customer, and the ability *to prove growth* to a customer.

Authority on Application

Branders must posture themselves as the applications authorities in the customer's industry. This is their prior certification. Applications authority presumes two capabilities. One is a knowledge of the customer's business: knowing the "what" about a customer. The second is a knowledge of implementation: the "how" about installing a product or system in a customer's operations. To know the what without the how is to be an academic. To attempt the how without knowing the what is to be a do-it-yourself brain surgeon.

In order to be an expert at applying a product or system to a customer's business functions, branders must be skilled at four things. (1) They must have entry skills so they can penetrate an operating process at the proper point, one of the 20 percent of its cost clusters or sales opportunities that yield 80 percent of the results. (2) They must have installation skills so they can integrate their product or system with a customer's ongoing operations, disrupting them minimally. (3) They must have migration skills so they can progressively optimize a customer's operations by adding to them new products or services or an upgraded system. And (4) They must have measurement skills so they can prove that the customer's productivity and profits are being increased according to plan.

There is no escape from application. That is what branders are paid for. Without application, profits can only be talked about. Application can make them happen. The ability to put expertise to work, to install it together with a product or service system in a customer's business and make profits as a result, is the branders' artistry. It defines their relationship with customers. It answers the question, why do business with the high-priced supplier? It reminds branders what business they are in and directs their attention and resources to their true assests—knowledgeable people.

Authority on Education

Branders must also posture themselves as the education authorities in the customer's industry. This is their companion certification to applications authority.

Resultful appliers, ones who can prove that they improve customer profit, will be sought after on two grounds. One will be invitations to apply themselves to other customer businesses; to do for them what they have demonstrated they can do for others. The other will be invitations to teach customer people how to internalize the branders' expertise.

How can a customer's work force keep down the costs that branders can reduce? How can they maintain improved productivity, suppress downtime, keep receivables collected, forecast more exactingly, or balance inventory more optimally? Also, how can they keep up the sales revenues that the brander can increase? How can they continue to grow their own customers, substantiate premium prices, and concentrate on high-level decisionmakers?

Branders must be not only good appliers. They must be good

teachers of how application must be made to produce improved profits. If they cannot teach, they will have no multiplier of their ability to make a financial impact on customer businesses. As soon as they have finished their application, the value of their contribution would begin an immediate decline when customers regained sole control of their enhanced business functions. Operationally, they would be demonstrably better. But as profit improvers, the branders' systems would be diminishingly effective with time.

Training not only accelerates a customer's learning curve. It helps assure that there will be one. It gives customers proprietorship of their systems for improving profit: They become "ours" and not "theirs," the brander's. As customers become trained in improving their profits, they can put a knowledgeable value on their partnership with their branders. They will want to protect and preserve it. More important, they will want to grow it. Once having experienced the value of an incremental dollar, they will want more.

So important are the branders' needs to be training authorities that teaching and learning must be the cyclical rhythm of their partnerships. They must teach what they know. They must learn the rest. The more they teach, the more they will learn; every solution reveals the next problem. The more they learn, the more opportunity they will find to teach. What they learn will compose their databases. What they teach will compose their proposals to improve customer profits.

The brand relationship begins with teaching. The branders' initial approach to a customer is based on sharing something the branders know. It may be something quite specific about the customer's business. Or it may be a generality, a norm, about the customer's industry in a category where the branders believe a customer to be deficient.

From that moment on, branders are always in a teaching role. They bring new information constantly to the surface: Look at what is going on in this or that operation; look at the progress in improving its contribution. They counsel on what options for improvement exist and recommend the option of choice: What if we go with this one because it represents the optimal solution?

They audit, analyze, and review results, making their lessons clear. They draw up their operational curriculum so that old hands can be reinforced and new-hires informed about the whys and wherefores of what they have done, for only they will be able to perpetuate it.

Branders build monuments in their customer businesses. They are not systems. They are people, customer people who take over the branders' skills and thereby free them to migrate onto successive problems where they will again apply and educate, teach and learn.

Authority on Proof

Branders do not say, "Trust me. Take my word." They say, "Partner me. Take my profits." They do not ask for acts of faith. They present acts of proof. Adept at quantifying their results, branders put numbers on their contributions so that their significance can be judged. The customer may wonder, Is the brander doing the job, earning the premium pay? The proof is in the profits. Is the brander's contribution still coming in, or was the brander just a hotshot one-shot? The proof is in the profits. What is the brander worth to us; how can we get a fix on the true value? The proof is in the profits.

Branders' norms arm them with proof of what they can do. They give conjecture some boundaries. But branders must prove something more than what they have done. They must prove they are capable of doing it anew with each customer. And they must prove it each time. Because branders ask premium prices, branders live in the world of "What have you done for me lately?" The customer's investment will always be considered too high unless the return is even higher again and again.

The branders' best friend is their cost-benefit analysis of a customer's business. It shows the benefits in terms of incremental profit as a return on incremental investment. Here is where you are now, the cost-benefit analysis reveals. Here are your current costs or sales. Here is where you will be in return for this incremental investment. Here is your current bottom line: net profit before tax and rate of return. Here it is again after our proposal.

This is the benefit, the value added by doing business with a brander.

The cost-benefit analysis proves the value of branders' authoritativeness in applications expertise and as educators. It declares straightaway exactly how much in authority they really are. It demonstrates to the customer not how much they know but how much of it they can pay off; not how much they have learned but how much of it they can teach.

Branders are constantly in a state of proof. There are four stages. First, before they can create a brand partnership, branders must prove that they have a track record. They have already improved someone's profit, preferably in a customer's own industry or an industry the customer can relate to. The best proof is case history proof. Through customer testimonials, the branders' capabilities are proclaimed for them. Testimonials tell how customers have become "best" as a result of partnering with their branders. That is why, when branders advertise, they never write a word of their own. Their customers speak for them. They speak in customer language, the only language that other customers understand. It is not the language of high-pressure sales persuasion. It is the language of high-level profit improvement.

After branders prove their track record, they enter the second stage of proof. As a result of applying their capabilities to solve customer problems and help seize customer opportunities, branders become smart. They become process-smart about customer cost problems and market-smart about customer sales opportunities.

They learn average costs on a process-by-process basis. They learn the value of decreasing them by each successive percentage point. They learn the average investment it requires and the return that can be expected. The same is true for sales. Branders learn the average dollar value of each market share point on a market-by-market basis. They learn the value of increasing it by each successive percentage point. They learn the average investment it requires and the return that can be expected. They must teach these industry averages, the brander's "norms," to their customers to prove they know the customers' industries.

But industry knowledge of and by itself is never sufficient.

The brander's third stage of proof must show customers why industry norms are important to them as yardsticks against which their own performance can be measured. Here is the average cost contributed by this business function: Are you above it or below it? If you are above, what is it worth to drop it closer to the norm? What will you have to invest to do it? What will be your return? Here is the average sales revenue contributed—or potentially contributable—by this market segment: Are you above it or below it? If you are below, what is it worth to raise it closer to the norm? What will you have to invest to do it? What will be your return?

What if a customer is better than the norm? The customer has three options: (1) leave well enough alone and go on to something else, (2) safeguard the present superiority, or (3) increase it even more, further improving its contribution to profit.

In this third stage of proof, branders are showing customers that they know something about the customers' businesses. They know where customers are long on costs or short on sales revenues, either from their homework or from what customers will teach them in response to industry norms. They know how to shorten the costs where they are long and to lengthen the sales revenues where they are short. Because they know the customer's business and not just their own, they can earn the right to consult on its improvement.

The fourth and final stage of the branders' proof comes when they prove that they have a control system. It must progressively monitor the partners' progress in improving customer profit. It must also prove the profit is being improved according to plan.

We have done it successfully before, we have the industry norms as a result, we know how your business compares against them, we can measure our ability to improve your performance— these are the proofs that branders must present to ensure customer acceptance of their brand posture. Armed with customer testimonials that fulfill the requirements for the first two stages of proof, plus a cost-benefit analysis that fulfills the last two stages of proof, branders are ready to take their positions. Somewhere below them, "downstairs" in the customer hierarchy, vendors who compete against branders are presenting proof of their products' performance and warrantee fulfillment. In this way, they, too, take their positions.

How Branders Know They Are Branded

Branders know they are branded by the way their customers come to them. If customers make product inquiries, a would-be brander is exposed as a vendor in brand clothing. True branders are addressed according to their authoritativeness. You have my industry norms, customers will say. You can tell what our own numbers ought to be, based on them. You can tell us if we're overcosted. You'll know where we're leaving money on the table in our key markets. Can you come in and look us over? Tell us what improvements we can expect. How much? How soon? How sure?

You have the applications expertise, customers will say. You know how to enter our major business functions at the points where their key cost clusters are located. You know how to work with our people to reduce those costs. You also know how to help us penetrate our key markets more quickly, more deeply, and more profitably. You can do these things with greater cost-effectiveness and less disruption to our business than we can do them ourselves—or than anyone else can do them. Because we are prepared to believe that you can do more for us, we are prepared to pay you more.

When premium price is no object—when premium value is the only object—branders have the ultimate way of knowing that they are branded. Their customers will become better business managers. They will have learned some of the branders' process-smarts and market-smarts. Their customers will be richer. They will be able to pay their branders another round of premium prices for another round of premium values. Their customers will be prouder, too: proud enough of being "best" to provide their branders with another testimonial to their posture.

Appendix C

Technology Venturing to Assure Future Competitiveness

Recompetitiveness renews the lease on life of the Big Winner businesses of the near-term past. What about the Big Winner businesses of the near-term future? How can managers assure themselves of a sufficient supply of candidate opportunities in the emergent growth technologies that will provide the commercial foundations of the next cycle of branded mainstream businesses?

A number of corporations have adopted a process for improving their chances for coming up with Big Winners on a planned basis, not as a once-in-a-generation dark horse but as a predictable cyclical event. To accomplish their objective, they have fortified themselves with three capabilities:

1. Access to emergent developmental technologies that can serve as the capability bases of highly profitable new businesses.
2. Knowledge of high-added-value market applications for these technologies.
3. A method for validating and ranking the most profitable business concepts linking the technologies to their market applications.

These capabilities can assure opportunities. In order to implement them, two other requirements must be met: a flexible mix of strategies for moving the most likely business concepts into timely commercialization, and a cadre of trained entrepreneur managers to run internally developed businesses or work with external companies as partners or joint venturers.

Positioning Emergent Technologies

Growth is almost always spoken of as if it were a unitary strategy. A company that pays venture capital firms to bird-dog acquisition candidates and then buys into one or two of them from time to time, says that it is a "growth company." Another business that funds its own internal entrepreneurs and may set them up as spun-off subsidiary organizations also calls itself a growth company. Other businesses support technological discovery in freewheeling think tanks like skunk works, or joint venture with other companies' scientists, and claim equal consideration as growers.

All are correct. Yet each strategy is only a single module in the comprehensive growth universe that, as Figure C-1 shows, consists of three rings.

1. Logical extensions of base-business technologies that lead to the acquisition of corollary sciences or product migrations from the mainstream foundations of a business. IBM's branching out of data processing technology by ac-

Figure C-1. The growth universe.

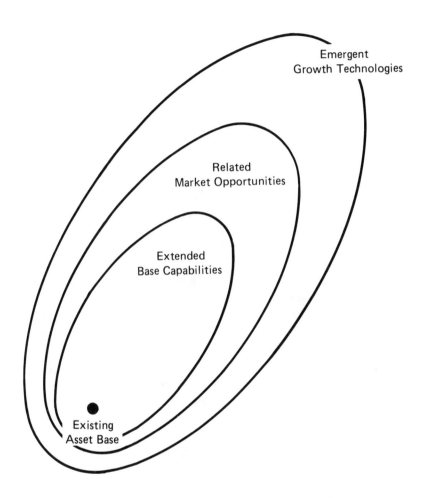

quiring the compatible telecommunications capabilities of
Rolm is an example of logic in growth extension.

2. Market applications of existing technologies that permit
   penetration into related or even wholly removed customer
   segments. General Motors has made minority investments
   in artificial intelligence and robotics that will enable it to
   serve markets for automated manufacturing systems that

are independent of, yet can be related to, its traditional automotive business.

3. Emergent growth technologies that can represent the businesses of the future and may therefore have no relationship to current core technologies or existing markets.

The emergent growth technologies of the near-term future, those in the third ring, cover a lot of ground. They include computer applications to manufacturing called flexible manufacturing systems, some controlled by artificial intelligence software and operating with robotics instead of human labor. Within artificial intelligence itself, there are databases of expert knowledge and applications in the form of training programs or diagnostic protocols. Smart robots are obtaining sensory enhancements that enable them to possess vision, acute tactile sensitivity, and voice activation. In the biotechnologies, recombinant DNA and monoclonal antibodies can diagnose and fight disease and alter plant, animal, and human life. New Space Age materials that combine unique strength, lightness, and temperature tolerance promise to replace many of the plastics and metals of the Industrial Age.

Some of the new opportunity areas offer intriguing combinations of seemingly unrelated technologies. Bioelectronics, as an example, incorporates biology with electronics to produce biochips as an alternate power source to silicon microchips. Similar hybrid business opportunities reside in the spaces between other sciences.

If areas like these seem too exotic, more prosaic targets closer to home may be represented by new generations of electronic process controls, biotechnological applications to cleanup of industrial waste or spillage, or even consumer uses for industrial or military technologies like the personal computer and transistor.

Adding emergent technologies to the growth process means that no single strategy is being solely relied on to provide new sources of profits. Instead, a comprehensive development program is in place. Under it, core technologies are being extended through internal research and development as well as R&D partnerships, joint ventures, and acquisitions. New market applications are occurring by means of sales and marketing partnerships along with internally generated venture businesses and toehold or foothold acquisitions. And finally, investments and partnerships are being made to establish capabilities in emergent growth.

Growth Cycles for Big Winners

The process for growing Big Winners has two objectives for each growth cycle. One is a hit ratio of one Big Winner from every eight candidates. The other is a survival-to-loss ratio of three profitmaking survivors for every two whose profits are lost to breakeven or failure. Achieving these two ratios tells us that the process is working.

The One-in-Eight Hit Ratio

In order to be cost-effective, the minimum yield of a growth cycle must be at least one valid Big Winner from every batch of eight alleged Big Winners. This will enable growth to be fairly predictable, reasonably consistent and largely self-financing through the recycling of profits. It will also allow growth to become familiar, making it the rule rather than an exception. If the mean time between Big Winners is stretched thinner than one in eight, growth becomes chancy and sporadic; it loses its rhythm as a planned, periodic event and may never be able to catch up paying back its development costs from profits.

Out of every cycle's eight growth candidates, each an alleged Big Winner, a maximum of three can be lost between the time the refinement process starts and the final cut begins. Of the five survivors we are left with, the most likely result, which is shown in Figure C-2, is as follows:

- *One Big Winner.* A new business with a minimum 30 percent annual rate of growth over its first three years and a minimum annual gross revenue of $25 million by year three.

Figure C-2. One-in-eight hit ratio.

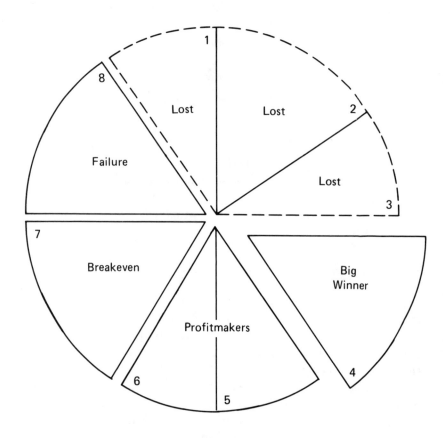

- *Two profitmakers.* New businesses with lower annual rates of growth and a lesser annual gross revenue contribution.
- *One breakeven business.* A new business that pays back its investment without contributing a positive return.
- *One failure.* A new business that does not achieve break-even by year three.

This can be looked at as a statement of sources and distribution of growth funds. The Big Winner and the two profitmakers are the profit sources for each growth cycle. The Big Winner's funds are the prime source of expanded corporate earnings. The new income from the two profitmakers pays for the cycle's in-

vestment, allowing it to be internally financed. The two remaining businesses, the breakeven and the failure, are costs. The breakeven business is an opportunity cost. The failure is a direct cost.

The Three-to-Two Survival-to-Loss Ratio

At each phase of a growth cycle, refinement takes place. When the cycle begins, all the candidates look good. On a judgmental basis, it is often hard to choose between them; all eight may look like Big Winners, thereby encouraging a euphoric "bonanza psychology" among management that will swiftly be disabused at the cycle's first turn.

After the cycle's first phase of screening, six of the original eight growth candidates should survive and two should be lost. After the second phase of testing, five of the surviving six candidates should still be survivors while one more candidate should be lost. Finally, after commercialization, three of the five candidates should be moneymakers and the other two should be losers. Figure C-3 shows that, of the three moneymakers, one can be the Big Winner.

This survival-to-loss experience acts like a probability curve to dictate the need for cranking up each growth cycle with eight prime candidates. No lesser number will yield the three moneymakers. Nothing less than truly prime candidates will survive the winnowing process to yield the one Big Winner. Unless there is a continuing supply of premier business opportunities to put into the hopper, management will be unable to count on producing a Big Winner from each development cycle. As either the quantity of candidates diminishes or their quality decreases, the odds against winners rise automatically.

Management Proprietorship

Corporate development begins when top management becomes its proprietor. Growth, in common with all policy decisions, starts at the top or it does not start at all. But developers cannot simply

Figure C-3. Three-to-two survival-to-loss ratio.

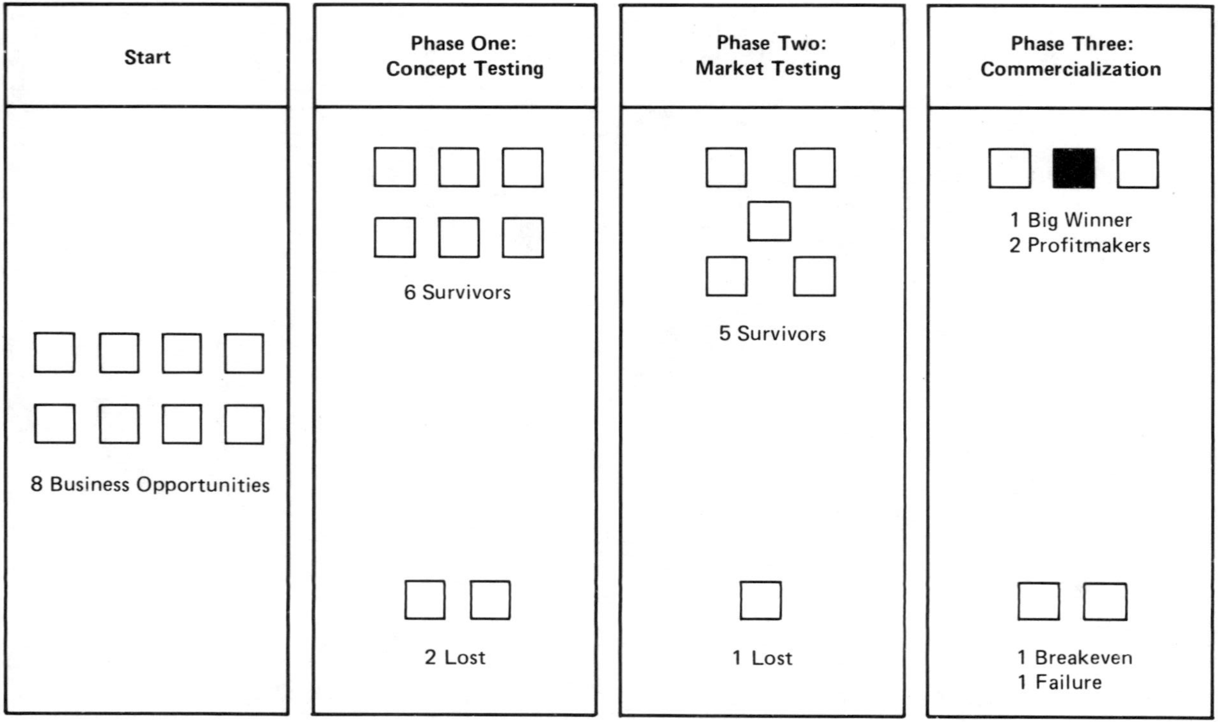

Start	Phase One: Concept Testing	Phase Two: Market Testing	Phase Three: Commercialization
8 Business Opportunities	6 Survivors	5 Survivors	1 Big Winner / 2 Profitmakers
	2 Lost	1 Lost	1 Breakeven / 1 Failure

await authorization; they must take aggressive action and lobby for it, testing and affirming the three pillars of top-level proprietorship.

1. *Criteria.* What does "growth" mean to management: how many new net dollars, at what rate, and over what time frame? What domains represent acceptable growth that will be compatible with a growth-oriented corporate concept of "fit"?
2. *Capabilities.* Is the internal resource base adequate to provide the requisite technological and marketing support for growth development? If not, will management make the investment?
3. *Commitment.* How well prepared is the company to implement growth opportunities as they are developed? Are sufficient funds available, are entrepreneur managers being trained, and are incentive-based compensation policies in place for them?

A top management that is ready to grow will signal its disposition. It will take affirmative action in formulating true stretch criteria, and it will make a visible commitment to a cadre of growth drivers and supportive resources for them—all in advance of receiving its first business opportunity. The up-front investments these acts certify are management's down payment on growth. To the extent that growth is a self-fulfilling prophecy, these acts are as essential psychologically as they are organizationally.

Process

If management's criteria for growth make sense and if its capabilities and commitment are strong, the six phases of the Big Winner development process can take place. The process is shown in

Figure C-4. Big Winner process.

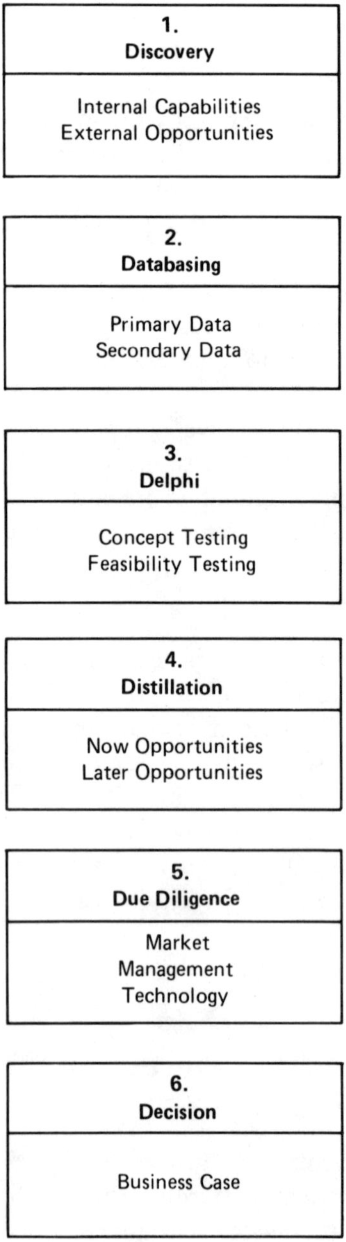

1.
Discovery
Internal Capabilities External Opportunities

2.
Databasing
Primary Data Secondary Data

3.
Delphi
Concept Testing Feasibility Testing

4.
Distillation
Now Opportunities Later Opportunities

5.
Due Diligence
Market Management Technology

6.
Decision
Business Case

Figure C-4. Its culmination will be a business case from which a market penetration plan can be drawn.

Phase 1: Discovery

The discovery of new business opportunities based on emergent technologies takes two forms: an internal search for opportunities that can be generated by corporate technologies, and an external search of posssible opportunities from a global brain bank.

Internally, two things should be looked for. The first is the potential to migrate a mainstream science into growth areas. The second is the existence of a renegade technology hiding out among the bunsen burners and bread boards, being pursued as a zealous vigil by a single individual or a hardy band during lunch hours, evenings, and weekends. From these scientists-in-hiding can come the deviations from corporate mainstreams that lead to winning commercializations.

On a global basis externally, a brain bank must be formed of leading doers, thinkers, and devil's advocates in emergent technologies and their market applications. Typical brain banks include inventors, scientists, incipient entrepreneurs in precorporate business groups, business analysts, government agency experts, business, trade, and professional association leaders, consultants, venture capital and other financial agents for new technology-based businesses, and industry-watchers in the United States, Western Europe, and the Pacific Basin countries.

The function of the brain bank is to act as the authoritative source of primary data on technologies. They are the horse's mouth. From them can be learned all that is knowable. What is a new science composed of? What other technologies does it draw from—what are its most likely migrations? What other technologies complement it or compete with it? What are its principal commercial applications—with what market segments, yielding what benefits to meet what needs at what probable value-to-price ratios? When will it be marketable? Who are its best developers; its best managers; its heaviest sponsors?

Phase 2: Databasing

Through personal interviews, mail, and telephone, the brain bank's knowledge, activities, and opinions are collated into a database on emergent technologies that are relevant to corporate growth objectives. These data are supplemented with secondary information from a global search of publicly available sources from individuals, institutions, government publications, and libraries.

The database may be thought of as a central repository of the raw materials from which future businesses can be made. Once amassed, they must be fashioned into business concepts: beneficial values that are expressed as if they were already deliverable— prepositioning statements for potential businesses.

In Figure C-5 an elementary concept statement is shown. It will undergo progressive enhancement if it attracts brain bank interest, having value added to it by the inclusion of cost-benefit analyses of operating benefits, bench test results, model advertisements, and eventually in-use tests of prototype systems.

Phase 3: Delphi

Through a serial process of iteration and reiteration, business concepts are circulated by the Delphi method through the brain bank. An ever-narrowing evaluation is sought for each concept: What are its perceived assets and liabilities, how do they compare with competitive concepts, what is the relative likelihood of their Big Winner commercialization, their most probable time frame, and most likely market composition? Markets themselves, once they have been identified, can also participate in the Delphi phase.

First by relatively broad-scale exposure, then by successively more vertical market niching, the most likely user segment will be sought. This will be a user group whose needs are sufficiently met by the business concept's technical capability to yield operating and financial benefits that merit a premium price. Without a sizable group of such users, there can be no Big Winner. Finding several small groups, or groups who perceive only minimal benefits, is no substitute for a single, significantly benefited user clus-

Figure C-5. Model concept statement.

Batch production of customized products as small as single units can now be cost-effectively manufactured, even in between mass-production runs. Switchover and switchback can be automatically accomplished within 100 nanoseconds, reducing downtime for all practical purposes to zero. Productivity is improved an average of 5 to 7 percent while costs can be reduced up to $10,000 per shift. These results are accomplished by a flexible manufacturing system that employs computerized robots guided by expert system software. The FMS work stations require maintenance on the average of once every 100,000 hours and need no human attendants to operate, service, or change programs. An FMS of this type can be installed on line for approximately $100,000 and can return the investment in full within six months.

ter. Nor is a propensity to buy cheap, even in volume, a suitable substitute for a premium price.

The classic mistake to be avoided is the one made by IBM for its PCjr. IBM, by its own admission, misjudged who would buy it and how much they would be willing to pay. Given these two errors, nothing could have made the PCjr a Big Winner.

Concept statements, concept advertising, and pro forma cost-benefit projections allow great flexibility in testing multiple solutions to the same market opportunity. Their downside comes from eliciting hypothetical responses to their patently unreal proposals. Prototype products can bring the real world closer but pay a price in flexibility. They are what they are, warts and all, and they may therefore narrowly focus critique on their specific configuration and performance rather than the broader concept they are intended to represent.

Phase 4: Distillation

The highest priority business concepts, each representing an emergent technology and its market applications, are ranked in an order of "now opportunities"—business opportunities worthy of immediate involvement through minority investment, joint venturing, or R&D partnering—and "later opportunities" that may require further study and lengthier tracking.

Phase 5: Due Diligence

Each entrepreneurial group, whether precorporate or actually in business, that offers a "now opportunity" must be evaluated to determine how partnerable, acquirable, or investable it is. Due diligence should focus on three primary growth factors, key characteristics that have been found to best predict fast, profitable growth: (1) management, in terms of its personal and professional background, leadership in technical skills, and commitment to growth; (2) the market, in terms of its projectable growth potential; and (3) the technology, in terms of its leading-edge nature, time and dollar costs of commercialization, comparative cost-effectiveness, barriers and constraints to life cycle growth, predictable obsolescence rate, and derivative technologies and applications.

Phase 6: Decision

A business case can now be prepared on each emergent opportunity. It will serve as the platform for a growth plan. The case states the facts about a business. It defines its technology base, market segmentation, product lines and their value-to-price relationships, and competitive and economic influencing factors. It discusses decision criteria for entry, such as richness, readiness, and reasonableness in relationship to business fit. A plan based on it will be able to calculate the growth that can be brought to the case and the preferred method for acquiring the opportunity.

Anticipating Problems

Fit versus Futures

A primary criterion for growth with most mature businesses is fit—their insistence on a logical connection between existing base businesses and anything new. More often than not, this means that the technology must be familiar. A chemicals processor, for example, sees a fit with hydrocarbon processing while electronic data processing is viewed as an alien science. Almost every *Fortune* 500 company can show scars that prove the validity of sticking to one's own knitting as far as growth is concerned. During the diversification craze of the 1970s, technology fit was subordinated as a growth standard for considerations of countercyclical cash flow or quick speculative return. Because there was no inherent glue to bind disparate business—and because it was discovered that there is no such animal as "a good manager who can manage anything"—the frenzy to diversify has led directly to a correlative frenzy to divest.

No one is anxious to repeat this process, which is costly in resources, repute, and human suffering. As a result, top management frequently asks for four to six new businesses over a five-to seven-year time frame that "fit within the realm" of the current business. Giant steps, no matter how inviting, are discouraged even when they can be taken with minimal risk. Instead, management lets it be known that growth begins—and ends—"a half step removed" from where the business is perceived to be today. This is the time-honored way by which commodity-based mature businesses produce commodity-based new businesses.

Taking half steps to growth is a necessary component of a comprehensive growth process. It enables a business to keep up with the natural evolution of its technologies and the changes in its markets' segmentation. Linked to the sponsorship of internal venturers who come to management for funds to commercialize their own ideas, logical extension helps make sure that the asset base of the business, already bought and paid for, is being fully capitalized and insured against opportunity loss. But fit-based strategies have one other attribute in common as well. Neither separately nor together are they likely to produce a true Big Winner business for the future.

Today's corporate realm is yesterday's future, not tomorrow's. While it is demonstrably possible to develop a handful of close-fit businesses that will cumulatively yield after-tax earnings of, let us say, $50 million by year five or seven, it is almost impossible to produce one business that will make such a contribution by itself or, in the manner of a Big Winner, exceed it. This is the difference between going for the home run or going for singles. While it is true that three singles can equal a home run, and that they are presumably easier to make, the home runs are largely concentrated in the emergent business of the future. This is home-run country. If management wants to be a leader of the future, there is no substitute for swinging for the fences.

By definition, growth into emergent technologies cannot fit within today's existing realm. This is its proof of being emergent. Some companies abide by a rule of thumb that warns, "If it fits, it's probably already mature." They base their thinking on the belief that businesses, like people, pass along a genetic inheritance to their offspring. Some of the deterministic code may be technological: A science may have lost its ability to commercialize products at Big Winner margins. Other codes may be market-connected: A market may be declining in size, altering its propensity to purchase or using only price as its buying guide. Representing half steps from their parent business, offspring with the same heredity are generally preordained to replicate their parental competitiveness for margins and market share with the same unspectacular results that encouraged their conception in the first place.

Eight-Barrel Pumpers

The ability to come up consistently with one Big Winner out of every eight new business opportunities depends on three factors:

1. A process for creating a continuing supply of high-quality opportunities to feed into the wide end of the hopper.
2. A process for testing the likelihood of each opportunity as a potential Big Winner profit producer.
3. A corps of trained entrepreneur managers who can realize the full profit of each Big Winner opportunity.

Success starts at the top. The productivity of the testing process and the impact of the entrepreneur managers clearly depend on the opportunities that are presented for testing and, if they survive, for management. There must be enough of them. They must each possess above-average intrinsic values. Unless their supply can be ensured, mediocrity will become inherent in corporate development. New businesses will be developed but they will overwhelmingly be what the oil industry calls eight-barrel pumpers—marginal profitmakers that cannot be dismissed as dry holes yet never fulfill the expectation that someday they will become gushers.

Eight-barrel pumpers are the bane of corporate development. They clog the system, investing irreplaceable management resources without commensurate return and preventing the pursuit of true Big Winners. Their opportunity cost is incalculable. Even after mediocrity has become obvious, each is protected by an advocacy that acts to postpone its disposition. Meanwhile, the euphoria of seeming to grow multiple new businesses deceives top management into complacency about its readiness for the future.

No major company requires, or can cope with, a large number of marginally profitable development businesses. A system that generates them is riddled with cost-ineffectiveness from its inception. Yet many corporations invite this very result. They operate without a method explicitly designed to deliver Big Winners. Instead, they solicit broad-scale ideas from their own people, funding them almost randomly or they spin out internal support services into free-standing subsidiary businesses. These models can be useful supplements to a Big Winner growth strategy. But wholesale dependence on them only assures the appearance of growth without its substance.

Half Stepping

To stop short of reaching out to the emergent sciences is to truncate the development process by limiting it to the markets and sciences of yesterday and today. What is considered "new" by a developing company may be the long-established domain of competitors. Simply introducing an innovation as "the new kid on the block" earns little or nothing. Only by breaking out into yet-uncompetitive arenas where ingenuity and insight are key determinants of success and where markets are up for grabs can the constraints imposed on premium margins by maturity be overcome.

In order to be a prominent player in the arena of emergent technologies, development managers must understand their unique role in the growth process. While most companies could well say, "We're not growing half as well as we know how," growth should not be allowed to become a serial function.

A policy of logical extension by half steps first, followed by market amplification in full steps and finally a giant step or two into emergent technologies is an infinite postponement of winning big for the future. It is practically a guarantee that current core businesses will remain the chief corporate dependence, accounting for 80 percent or more of annual profits while new businesses never achieve more than 3 to 5 percent. In sunset industries whose base businesses have long ago lost their thrust as high profit sources, deferring entry into emerging sciences can be fatal if there is nothing to take their place when what Du Pont has called "the end of the rainbow" is passed. For industries and businesses not yet at sunset, but where dusk and twilight are deepening, emergent technologies may be the only survival strategy other than downsizing or a friendly takeover.

The question for corporate development is not either-or but what is an optimal mix of the three basic growth strategies: logical extension from existing base capabilities, penetration of related market opportunities, and investment in emergent growth technologies. The minimal daily requirements for adding emergent technologies to the development process are few. Major up-front commitments are unnecessary. The General Motors model of minority investment, sometimes in more than one approach to the same science, restricts most involvements to a 20 percent ownership of emergent businesses. Other companies prefer partnerships and joint ventures to minority buy-ins, sometimes linking them up to internal development. No matter how they do it, growth companies have one attribute in common: They are growing throughout the growth universe, touching all the bases.

Consume or Supply: Make Money or Spend It

With maturity comes myopia, a foreshortening of the corporate vision. Huge sales volumes, dominant shares of market and mammoth asset bases bias managers to protect, preserve, and defend their core businesses to the detriment, if not the exclusion, of all else. The tips of their noses come to define the extent of their sightedness of the future. As their businesses age and products become margin-sensitive in the manner of commodities, restructuring along more emergent lines offers a way out.

The decision faced by all mature corporations is whether to be a maker or spender of money: either becoming a consumer of emergent technologies or a supplier. If top managers choose to consume, they will always be on the buying end of incorporating new sciences into their venerable processes to reduce cost or improve productivity—their attempt, in defiance of the odds, to stay competitive. Unfortunately, the only guarantee that comes with staying competitive is the chance to play the next round of technical upgrading with its attendant higher investment and risks. The option to be a supplier of emergent technologies, however, offers the only true opportunity to upgrade profits.

Even if it is managed insidiously, through technology creep, the infusion of emergent technology can give a business the chance to be born again. New technologies bring with them a recompetitive effect. They involve new people and new organization forms. They require new distribution systems, new sales strategies, and a confrontation with new customer decisionmakers. Older managers get a second chance to climb a rising curve. For new managers, the excitement of growing mainstream businesses of the future provides an incentive that recreates the vision of the founders, not to mention the chance, like them, to strike it rich.

Along with its effects on managerial life cycles, the exploitation of emergent technologies makes its major impact on the business life cycle itself. New S-curves—new businesses that can deliver truly innovative benefits—are what growth is all about: new profits unencumbered by mature margins, parity competition, saturated markets, or sated managers.

Glossary

Asset base The sum total of sunk costs for providing a capability to perform a business function.

Branding Creating a premium value, and creating a perception of that value in the minds of those who compose its market, that can command a premium price.

Brand stream A continuing flow of branded products, services, and systems timed so that new brands are commercialized before predecessor brands become mature.

Commodity A mature product, service, or system whose original differentiation has been replicated by competition so that it can no longer command a premium price.

Commodity-based business A business in which cash flow is dependent on the volume sales of low-margin, mature products, services, and systems.

Competitive maturity The recapture of competitiveness after maturity by rebranding products, services, and systems so that they can once again command a premium price.

Downward price management The progressive reduction of margins by a mature business as price becomes the sole competitive differentiation.

Knockoff A product, service, or system produced by competition that offers parity features and benefits at a lower price.

Margin control The ability to enforce a premium margin as a result of premium value, thereby maintaining control of profitability.

Mature market A market that is no longer growing, thereby requiring supplier growth to come from a tradeoff of market shares.

Noncompetitive maturity The inability or unwillingness to recapture competitiveness after maturity, characterized by continuing sales of commodity products on the basis of their price and performance.

Outsourcing Purchasing from a foreign or overseas-based supplier whose costs, especially in labor content, are lower.

Unitary strategy A master strategy that is focused on the single unifying objective of profit maximization.

Unit margin The key to profitability, representing the profit margin per each unit of product.

Volume-based business A business whose profit is dependent on maximizing the volume production and sale of low-margin products.

Volume capacity The maximum production that can be manufactured by existing plant and equipment.

Index

Index

system financing, 80–81

technical manager, on growth
    team, 57
technology, effect of, on
    maturation process, 11
technology licensing, as
    nongrowth strategy, 9
technology venturing, *see*
    emergent growth
    technologies
3M, and growth partnering, 22–23
three-to-two survival-to-loss ratio,
    growth strategy, 149, 150
time, devaluation power of, 132–
    133
training, brander's expertise in,
    137–139

Union Carbide, noncompetitive
    mindset of, 10
unitary strategy, definition of,
    164
unit margin
    branding and, 28
    definition of, 164
user differentiation, branding
    and, 129–130
    see also branding

use value, product value versus,
    31–32

value(s), types of:
    applied, 132
    future, 132–133
    investment, 132
    perceived, 31–32
value-to-price ratio,
    determination of, 79–
    80
vendor pricing, brand pricing
    versus, 35
volume, replacement of, with
    profit, 1–2
volume-based business
    definition of, 164
    marketing costs of, 42–44
    profit sources in, 47–48
volume capacity
    in competitively-mature
    business, 16
    definition of, 164

Xerox, reactions of, to market
    maturity, 7–8, 9
Xomox, recompetitive strategies
    of, 14